Guided Math in Action

Building Each Student's Mathematical Proficiency with Small-Group Instruction

Dr. Nicki Newton

Routledge
Taylor & Francis Group
New York London

First published 2013 by Eye On Education

Published 2013 by Routledge
711 Third Avenue, New York, NY 10017, USA
2 Park Square, Milton Park, Abingdon, Oxon OX14 4RN

Routledge is an imprint of the Taylor & Francis Group, an informa business

Library of Congress Cataloging-in-Publication Data

Newton, Nicki.
Guided math in action : building each student's mathematical proficiency with small-group instruction/Nicki Newton.
     pages   cm
ISBN 978-1-59667-235-2
1. Mathematics—Study and teaching (Elementary)
2. Group guidance in education.
3. Group work in education.
4. Effective teaching.
I. Title.
QA20.G76N49 2012
372.7—dc23   2012038646

Cover Designer: Dave Strauss, 3FoldDesign

ISBN: 978-1-596-67235-2 (pbk)

SFI Certified Sourcing
www.sfiprogram.org
SFI-00453

Printed and bound in the United States of America
by Edwards Brothers Malloy

Also Available from Eye On Education

**Using Formative Assessment
to Drive Mathematics Instruction in Grades PreK–2**
Christine Oberdorf & Jennifer Taylor-Cox

**Using Formative Assessment
to Drive Mathematics Instruction in Grades 3–5**
Christine Oberdorf & Jennifer Taylor-Cox

**Math in Plain English:
Literacy Strategies for the Mathematics Classroom**
Amy Benjamin

RTI Strategies that Work in the K–2 Classroom
Eli Johnson & Michelle Karns

**Math Intervention:
Building Number Power with Formative Assessments,
Differentiation, and Games (Grades PreK–2)**
Jennifer Taylor-Cox

**Math Intervention:
Building Number Power with Formative Assessments,
Differentiation, and Games (Grades 3–5)**
Jennifer Taylor-Cox

Engaging Mathematics Students Using Cooperative Learning
John D. Strebe

**Differentiated Instruction for K–8 Math and Science:
Ideas, Activities, and Lesson Plans**
Mary Hamm & Dennis Adams

**Family Math Night:
Math Standards in Action**
Jennifer Taylor-Cox

**Solving Behavior Problems in Math Class:
Academic, Learning, Social, and
Emotional Empowerment (Grades K–12)**
Jennifer Taylor-Cox

Supplemental Downloads

Many of the tools discussed and displayed in this book are also available on the Routledge website as Adobe Acrobat files. Permission has been granted to purchasers of this book to download these tools and print them.

You can access these downloads by visiting www.routledge.com/9781596672352 and click on the Free Downloads tab.

Acknowledgments

They say it takes a village to raise a child. It also takes one to write a book. I am so grateful to so many people for helping me along this journey. I would like to thank many people for their support, expertise, guidance, and encouragement during this project. First of all I would like to thank God, without him this would not be possible. Second, I would like to thank my mom, pa, bigmom, and granddaddy. Third, I would like to thank my family for all their love and support, especially my Tia that calls me every day to ask "What have you accomplished today?" My brother Marvin, sister Sharon and Uncle Bill provide a needed weekly contact to keep me on track.

Fourth, I would like to thank my staff that supports me all the time. I would like to extend a special thanks to Debra, Brittany, Gabby, Marline and Secoya for the help with the examples in the book. I would also like to thank George Davis for the Photos. I would like to thank the Ramirez family for allowing Chloe to be a model.

Fifth, I would like to thank all my friends who continually encourage me. I would like to especially thank Scott and Terri who let me stay at their house all the time, while I work in the city. This allows me to spend countless hours working on my manuscript! And they also feed me, to keep me going. Kimberly, Tracye, Tammy, Donna and Christine are some of my biggest cheerleaders.

Sixth, I would like to thank Bob for believing that this was going to get done because from the moment I brought him the project he could see it. I thank Heidi for recommending me to Bob. I thank Lauren for seeing me through the day-to-day process. I would also like to thank the reviewers for their feedback as well as the proofreader. Last but not least, I thank all the administrators, teachers and students that make my work possible and relevant.

About the Author

Dr. Nicki Newton has been an educator for more than 20 years, working in inner-city schools on both the East and West Coasts, with student populations ranging from pre-kindergarteners through doctoral students. Having spent the first part of her career as a literacy and social studies specialist, she built on those frameworks to inform her math work.

She has worked on developing Math Workshop and Guided Math Institutes around the country. Most recently, she has been helping districts and schools nationwide to integrate the Common Core State Standards for Mathematics and think deeply about how to teach these within a Math Workshop Model.

Dr. Nicki works with teachers, coaches, and administrators to make math come alive by considering the powerful impact that a small-group learning structure can have on student achievement. She is also an avid blogger (www.guidemath.wordpress.com) and Pinterest pinner (drnicki7).

Contents

1

Guided Math:
An Introduction

When I first started teaching, I met a master teacher named Coco Aguirre. She was loud and funny and really smart. She worked with her kids in small groups and taught them all how to read, write, and do arithmetic. A big sign over the threshold of her door said, "If kids don't learn the way you teach, then teach the way they learn." Simple but true. And so that's what I did.

Fortunately, the school that I landed my first teaching job in had an early bird–late bird structure. Half our kids came early in the morning and left about two, and then the other half came about an hour later and stayed late. The idea was to work with children in small groups for reading and math.

So I could say that this pathway of small guided math groups was laid out for me from the beginning. I believe that when you work with students in small groups, you reach them in a different way than in the whole group. You get to look straight in their eyes and listen carefully to each word that comes out of their mouths. You get to teach each one with a bit more intention than in the whole group. You get to invite each student to a front-row seat—as a participant, not a spectator.

Students get to get in the game, play hard, and learn lots. They each get to talk, to show their thinking, to question others, to engage deeply in rich mathematical conversations. They get to get on friendly terms with numbers, to take risks and to go from triumph to triumph at that kidney-shaped table. Here, in a guided math group, we foster mathematical thinkers, one problem at a time, in these small spaces. Guided math is an opportunity for teachers to provide specific mathematical interventions. Let's take a look now at one of those lessons in action.

A Guided Math Lesson in Action

Welcome to room 307. The class is in the middle of math workshop. It is the middle of the year and the students are working on place value. Mrs. Johnson has been working with her math coach to find meaningful ways to engage her second graders. Mrs. Johnson has a diverse class of students, so she has grouped them so that they are challenged according to their current skill level.

Mrs. Johnson is at the kidney table working with a novice-level guided math group. The students are in the middle of a chapter on two-digit subtraction and still struggling with understanding the idea of regrouping. Mrs. Johnson knows this from a look at their latest quiz. So, in this group, she is working on building conceptual understanding of two-digit subtraction. She has chosen to use the first level of manipulative with this group, meaning bundles of sticks, instead of a more abstract manipulative like base-ten blocks, which she uses with other groups. Each student has a bundle of sticks grouped in tens.

Introduction: Mini-Lesson

During the mini-lesson, Mrs. Johnson wants to tap into prior knowledge, grab the students' attention, and hook them into today's lesson. She also wants to make sure they have a handle on the vocabulary so they can describe their thinking in math language.

Mrs. Johnson: Hello, everyone. Today we are going to continue our work with subtraction. Who can tell me in your own words what subtraction means?

Tom: Take away.

Here, in this first question, Mrs. Johnson has tapped into prior knowledge, stressed vocabulary, and set the purpose for today's lesson.

Mrs. Johnson: Okay, would someone like to elaborate on that; say some more about subtraction?

Sue: It's like if I have 25 dolls and I give you 16, that's subtraction.

Mrs. Johnson: Okay, so today we will be practicing more subtraction problems. We will be using these bundles. Remember, we were using these the other day. They help us see how we break tens to get ones. What do the bundles represent?

Carol: They are tens.

Mrs. Johnson: And when they are loose sticks, what do we call them?

David: Those are the ones.

Mrs. Johnson: Everyone hold up a bundle of tens. Now, hold up enough bundles to make 30. Okay, now on your mats, put out enough bundles and ones to show what 45 looks like. Okay, now. Let's start with the problem Sue gave as an example. Say I have 25 dolls. Everyone show me enough tens and ones to represent 25. Okay, now I want to give 16 away. What do I need to do? Who can explain?

Maria: Well, you don't have enough ones to just take 6 away so you have to break a ten.

Mrs. Johnson: Thumbs ups if you agree, thumbs down if you don't, thumbs sideways if you are not sure. (She checks around and then continues.) Okay, who can explain what happens next?

Tom: If you break a ten, you have 1 ten and 15 ones.

Mrs. Johnson: So can I now take 16 away?

Carol: Yes, you take away 6 ones and you take away the ten. You have 9 left.

Mrs. Johnson: Okay, does everybody see that? Any questions? Okay, let's try another one together before you all do one by yourselves. Let's say I have 32 marbles. Everybody set that up. Okay, say I want to give 15 away. What do I do?

Maria: You have to break 1 bundle of ten. Now you have 12 ones and 2 bundles of ten. So you can take 1 bundle of ten and 5 ones. So there is 1 bundle of ten left and 7 ones. You have 17 left.

Mrs. Johnson: Does everyone agree with Maria? Okay, now I am going to give each one of you a problem and I want to watch you do it. Then I will have you explain it to the group.

Student Work Period

During the work period, the students work on the problems by themselves. Sometimes they work in pairs. The idea is that children get to do some independent practice after the guided practice. During the work period, the teacher checks in with the students, taking anecdotals and asking questions. Each student has two problems to solve. After they finish, they share their solutions with the group.

Kayla: My problem was 27 take away 9. I didn't have enough ones to take away 9, so I had to break the ten pack. Then I took 9 away and I had 18 left.

John: My problem was 21 take away 12. I counted the ones, but I didn't have enough to take away 2, so I broke the ten pack. I took away 1 ten pack and 2 ones. I had 9 left.

After everyone has a chance to share, Mrs. Johnson moves on to the next part of the lesson.

Share Period

The share period is a crucial part of the lesson. It is when the teacher concretizes the learning for the day. It is a time to facilitate more discussion about the math concepts, strategies, and ideas worked on and it is also a time to make clarifications, address confusions, and add other comments.

At the end of the share period, the teacher gives directions about the follow-up center work as well as differentiated homework specifically for this group. After everyone has a chance to share, Mrs. Johnson asks some closing questions.

Mrs. Johnson: So who can tell me what was the math we were working on?

Mike: Take aways.

Mrs. Johnson: Yes, we were taking away. What is another name for this?

Tyrone: Subtraction.

Mrs. Johnson: Who can explain what we were doing in order to subtract?

Kayla: We had to break the tens to get more ones.

Mrs. Johnson: Why?

John: Because there wasn't enough in the ones place.

Mrs. Johnson: Okay, so this group is going to work on the Race to Zero center. You know the game where you start with 50 sticks in bundles of 10 and you roll the dice and take that number away until you get to 0. For homework, you all will take a baggie of sticks and 10 subtraction problems to complete on the homework sheet.

Mrs. Johnson then dismisses this group and begins to circulate around the room where the other children are working on differentiated, standards-based center activities. At the first table, four children are working on subtraction problems with the number grid. They have 10 problems that they must use the number grid to help them solve. At the second table, six children are working in pairs. One person rolls two dice and makes the largest number possible and the other person must subtract ten. They can use the number grid or the number line as a resource. Then they check the answer with the calculator. At the third table, the children are working on the computer. They are working in pairs on base-ten activities from the National Library of Virtual Manipulatives. At the fourth table, the children are working at a "hot topics center" reviewing money. They are playing a money match card game in which they match the amount to the coins. At the fifth table, the children are playing a game in which they roll a number and add 10 more.

Mrs. Johnson walks around the room taking anecdotals on three children whom she has chosen to watch for the day. She is getting ready to give the Big Switch signal on the xylophone (which is her cleanup signal), so that all the children will quickly and quietly prepare to come to the rug to discuss their math work for the day. Mrs. Johnson writes a note to herself that tomorrow she should definitely do a math interview with Daniel about subtracting double-digit numbers because she thinks he might be ready to move to a more challenging group.

This scenario shows the benefits of a guided math group. Mrs. Johnson understands the benefits of differentiated, targeted, standards-based practice. In this structure, she has the flexibility to pull small groups and provide instruction at their current level of understanding while the other students stay engaged in meaningful practice in standards-based math centers.

Summary of the Guided Math Lesson

During this guided math lesson (see Figure 1.1, page 8), Mrs. Johnson worked with a group of struggling mathematicians to build conceptual understanding. Her focus for the lesson was for the students to get a hands-on feel for subtraction with two-digit numbers. This is very often taught at a procedural level, teaching students the steps to regrouping. However, often students know how to do it but cannot explain what they are doing. So, with this group, the teacher has not yet started to work with abstract numbers, but has rather focused on using a primary-level manipulative to build mathematical understanding of subtraction in the base-ten system. The introduction of her lesson took about five minutes. She led students through a series of guided problems, so they could talk out the steps together as they worked. The independent student work that followed the guided practice took about seven minutes. Here, the students practiced regrouping and applied this skill to new problems. They also had to explain their thinking. Then Mrs. Johnson concluded with a share period.

Goals of Guided Math

The goal of guided math is for students to become proficient mathematicians who have conceptual understanding, procedural fluency, strategic competence, adaptive reasoning, and mathematical confidence. Guided math aims to get students comfortable with numbers, operations, and mathematical concepts so they can independently work with them in new and different contexts. In guided math groups, students can work on developing content knowledge and "habits of mind" and "ways of doing" math.

In guided math groups, we group children by targeted areas of need in order to teach at each child's instructional level. Guided math is an interactive space where children are doing the math with each other, by themselves, and with the teacher. The teacher's main role is to watch, observe, coach, and assess. The teacher also models and prompts as the students work. During guided math, students work on "just right" problems in their zone of proximal development. The level of instruction is not too easy or too hard but "just right"—that is, just enough of a reach that students learn from each new mathematical encounter.

Students are placed in flexible, homogeneous groups according to their performance on a variety of mathematical assessments, depending on the

Figure 1.1 Mrs. Johnson's Guided Math Lesson Plan

Date: December 10, 2012

Group: Blue Trapezoids

Teaching Focus: Subtraction using regrouping

Vocabulary and Phrases:
Bundles of ten
Tens
Ones
Regrouping
Breaking a ten

Mini-Lesson:
Connect to prior knowledge
Reinforce vocabulary
Guided practice problems/Checking for understanding

Student Activity:
Students will solve their own problems using the manipulatives
Student must explain their work using math words

Share:
Reinforce procedure of regrouping
Reinforce vocabulary

Assessment:
Check each student's individual work
Also note ongoing conversation and contributions to overall discussion

Notes:
Carlos had trouble explaining what he did
Maria got confused on 37–29, but she was able to figure it out with guided
    questions

Center Activities:
Race to Zero and basic subtraction flash cards

Homework:
Take subtraction problems home with a stick bundle to use as
    manipulatives

current unit of study. Based on the assessments, specific teaching points are selected and the lessons focus on these.

Beliefs About Teaching and Learning Mathematics That Frame Guided Math

Meeting Students Where They Are

Guided math allows you to meet students where they are so you can take them where they need to go (see Figure 1.2, page 10). Guided math allows you to scaffold learning so that even if you are on page 72 of the math book, you can teach all the students what they need to be ready for the current concept. Let's say page 72 is teaching double plus one facts. You already know that some students aren't quite ready for this. Some students don't know their doubles. Some students don't even know their facts through ten. Some students don't even know their numbers!

A guided math structure allows you to pull students in small groups and teach them in their zone of proximal development (Vygotsky, 1978). We already know that everyone is not on the same page at the same time. Although all the students are working on the big idea within a particular math strand, they are working at their instructional level. For example, double plus one is a math strategy that comes up in a particular lineup of teaching math strategies. As a knowledgeable teacher, you would recognize the appropriate place in the sequence for each group of children and then group them accordingly. Thus, eventually everyone will learn doubles plus one facts, but you'll do first things first.

It might look like this in your classroom. If the class is working on addition, there might be four groups. Group 1 (novice learners) might be working on facts through ten with concrete scaffolds such as ten-frames. Group 2 (apprentice learners) might be working on fluency with doubles using double ten-frames. Group 3 (practitioner learners) might be working on facts through 20 using double ten-frames. Group 4 (expert learners) might be working on adding a double-digit number with a single-digit number.

Tapping into Multiple Learning Styles and Intelligences

Children's learning styles and intelligences are considered in the planning and implementation of guided math lessons. Diverse instructional strategies, integrating linguistic, musical, visual, logical-mathematical, digital, bodily-kinesthetic, interpersonal, and intrapersonal approaches are used (Gardner, 1983). Teachers should have a toolkit of songs, poems, chants, manipulatives, charts, diagrams, and various activities. You might teach the students a concept through a song one day and the next you might play

Figure 1.2 Beliefs About Teaching and Learning Mathematics

Beliefs About Students and Learning Math	Beliefs About Teachers and Teaching Math	Beliefs About Developing Mathematical Proficiency
Children learn at their own pace	Teachers need to have solid content knowledge	Math should be taught at the concrete, pictorial, and then abstract level
Children have different learning styles (visual, auditory, kinesthetic) that need to be addressed	Teachers need to make connections with real life by contextualizing all the math they teach	Math should be taught with an emphasis on conceptual understanding, procedural fluency, and problem-solving skills
According to Gardner's theory, children have dominant learning intelligences (logical-mathematical, musical, spatial, linguistic, naturalist, interpersonal, intrapersonal, bodily-kinesthetic)	Teachers need to find new ways to teach children, if the children are not learning the way the teachers are teaching	Math should be contextualized so it makes sense
All children can learn math	Teachers should provide some small-group guided math instruction	
Smart is learned (Resnick, 1999)	Teachers should differentiate learning (process, product, content) (Tomlinson, 2001, 2003; Tomlinson & Eidson, 2003)	
Affect must be acknowledged in the math learning process—because learning math can be very emotional	Teachers need to work with children to set specific learning goals	
Students should reflect on their knowledge bases and skill sets and should set personal math goals		
Fundamental belief: Every child has the right to become a flexible, competent, confident mathematician!		

with the base-ten blocks or represent problems by drawing pictures with different colored pencils.

Building Mathematical Confidence

Children's disposition toward math is considered and valued during the design of lessons. Children are taught to acknowledge and work through frustrating moments while learning to become confident mathematicians. You talk about how sometimes they have to "wrestle with the math problem." You talk about what it means to "stick with it." You talk about "stepping away for a minute" and then being sure to come back to the problem. In guided math groups, the children and the teacher discuss "what's tough" and "what's easy." Students talk about themselves as learners, what they "get" and what they are still in the "process of getting." Students become reflective learners who set goals for themselves.

Stretching Your Own Pedagogy

Running guided math groups effectively requires teachers to "stretch their own pedagogy" (Mulgrave, personal communication, 2011) so they can reach and teach all students. This really means that teachers reflect on their usual practice, take notes about what is working and what is not working, and then stretch out of their own zones of comfort in order to devise new and engaging ways to help everyone learn. It means that if Johnny doesn't get it after you've tried to teach him three different ways, then you try a fourth. You teach from your own dominant intelligences, and that works for some students and it doesn't for others. You have to make sure you are using a variety of strategies, not just the ones you like and know best.

Summary

Guided math provides a powerful opportunity for students to learn math. In small groups, you can meet learners where they are and take them to where they need to go. You get everyone talking to each other. You coach learning. You facilitate thinking. You orchestrate masterful conversations. Everyone is invited to engage as thinking mathematicians. Students get to hear how others are doing it, and they also hear themselves make sense of the math they are doing. They get immediate feedback so that they can stay on track. Guided math provides time for students to make more and more sense of math in its growing complexity at a pace that is appropriate for them. Guided math is good for all students. It allows them all to reach their next level.

Reflection Questions

1. Currently, do all the students in your class feel that they can learn math?
2. What do you do with the students who are frustrated?
3. Does everyone participate in mathematical conversations? Who does, how, and under what terms?
4. How do you promote perseverance in your classroom?

2

Guided Math
in a Numerate
Environment

Proving Your Thinking

The other day I was playing Fraction Bingo with a class of fourth grad-ers. There were a number of fractions on the board and the students had filled in a bingo grid with those numbers in a random order. As I called out a fraction, I would ask questions about it. When someone gave me a satisfactory answer, they could all mark their boards, and whoever got four corners plus the middle first could call bingo. So I asked which of the fractions on the board was closest to zero. One little girl eagerly raised her hand and with great assurance said, "One-eighth." Looking at her seri-ously, I asked, "Are you sure about that?" She lowered her hand and said quite confidently, "NO!"

I was in the middle of saying "Ah" when another student raised her hand and said, "She's right. I'm sure. Because the smaller the denomina-tor, the larger the fraction." I said, "Then why is $\frac{9}{10}$ not the answer?" She responded confidently, "No, $\frac{9}{10}$ is close to 1 because it is 9 out of 10 parts." I looked at the other little girl who had answered first, and I said, "You were right! But you've got to be able to prove it." She smiled and I went on to call out a different fraction.

I find that many students don't know how to defend their thinking or challenge the thinking of others. Guided math groups provide the perfect setting for students to work on these skills. You should post charts in your classroom showing ways to prove a claim and listing a series of thinking prompts (see Figures 2.1 and 2.2, page 16).

Guided math can happen in a variety of contexts. Whatever the context, whether you do math workshop or not, the atmosphere should be filled with talking and making mathematical sense (see Figure 2.3, page 17). Students should be ready for that famous phrase "Prove it" or "Show me what you know." The culture should support reasoning out loud. Students should realize that they have to explain and write about what they are thinking. In order to support this process, students should be in mathe-matically rich environments that support thinking in a variety of ways,

Figure 2.1 Prove-It Posters

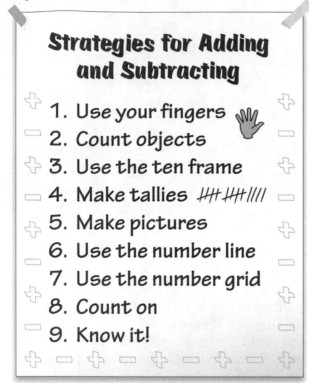

Strategies for Adding and Subtracting

1. Use your fingers
2. Count objects
3. Use the ten frame
4. Make tallies ℍℍ ℍℍ ////
5. Make pictures
6. Use the number line
7. Use the number grid
8. Count on
9. Know it!

Prove-it posters help students think! The posters provide prompts as to the ways students might prove their thinking.

Figure 2.2 Math Thinking Prompts

Why do you think that?	Are you sure about that?	Is that reasonable?	Who agrees?	Who disagrees?
Who got a different answer?	Why?	Explain your answer.	Prove it!	What strategy did you use?
Show us a model.	Convince us that you are right.	Who can explain this strategy?	Show two ways to do that.	Is that always true?

Figure 2.3 A Numeracy-Rich Environment

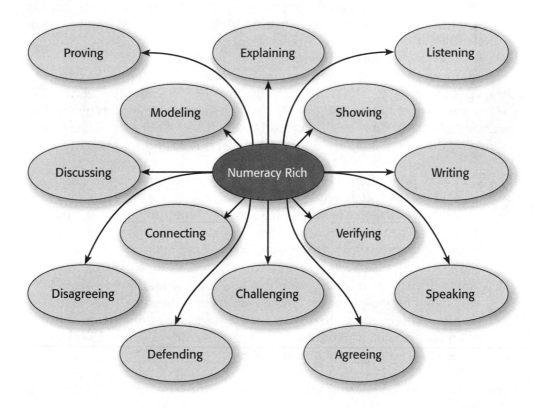

with concrete manipulatives, with counters, with graphic organizers (like number lines and grids), with drawings, or by acting it out.

Math Workshop

In a numeracy-rich classroom, children have a sense of community. According to Kohn (1996), a community is a "place in which students feel cared about and are encouraged to care about each other. They experience a sense of being valued and respected, the children matter to one another and to the teacher. They have come to think in plural; they feel connected to each other, they are part of an 'us'" (cited in Opitz, 1998). In a numeracy-rich classroom culture, children are taught to be respectful, to honor everyone's thinking, and to encourage each other. They respect the risk-taking challenge. They feel that they are all on the same team, so they can ask each other questions, challenge each other's ideas, share their thinking, and defend their thoughts. The place that provides this sense of belonging is the math workshop.

A math workshop classroom has several components. The important thing is to establish a very organized system in which most of the class is actively engaged in meaningful activity that they can do independently while the teacher pulls a guided math group. I am going to describe guided math within a math workshop because I highly recommend that we think about teaching math using a workshop model. In a workshop model, we take time to explore different elements of learning math.

Math workshop is a space where you make thinking visible. During the opening of the workshop, the small-group lessons, and the debrief, you have the opportunity to open up everyone's thoughts to each other. David Perkins (2003) emphasizes the importance of these public thinking rituals when he discusses "making thinking visible, public and permanent":

> Consider how often what we learn reflects what others are doing around us. We watch, we imitate, we adapt what we see to our own styles and interests, we build from there. Now imagine learning to dance when the dancers around you are all invisible. Imagine learning a sport when the players who already know the game can't be seen. Bizarre as this may sound, something close to it happens all the time in one very important area of learning: learning to think. Thinking is pretty much invisible. To be sure, sometimes people explain the thoughts behind a particular conclusion, but often they do not. Mostly, thinking happens under the hood, within the marvelous engine of our mind-brain. (p. 1)

So in math workshop, you are opening up your students' mathematical "mind-brains"!

Spaces and places are important for teaching and learning. In math workshop, there is a home base. This is some dedicated space in the room where support structures are evident, tools are handy, and thinking is recorded. Everyone gathers together in this space at the beginning to commence the journey of the day and at the end to summarize and share learning along the way. There should be math charts, white boards, number grids, number lines, interactive boards, anchor charts, poems, songs, chants, the class math journal, and all the other stuff you need to engage in fruitful mathematical discourse.

Home base is where the community members meet to gather their thoughts, share ideas, discuss topics, ask questions, and engage each other as public mathematicians in a community of learners. Often I encourage teachers to have students sit by a regular talking-thinking buddy. These buddies could be set for two weeks, a month, or a unit of study. It is good for students to pair up with someone to have an ongoing mathematical dialogue. As Harvey and Goudvis (2000) note, "Gathering kids in front for instruction, releasing them to practice, and then bringing them back to share their thinking represents the steady flow that is at the heart of effective teaching and learning" (p. 31).

Elements of a Math Workshop

Math workshop allows time to explore the calendar, time to work on strategic mathematical thinking, time to introduce and discuss the math for the day, and time for students to work in centers with partners and in groups. During this student activity time, the teacher works with a small guided math group. After student activity time, everyone comes back to a central location to discuss the day's activities in a whole-group share. Figure 2.4 shows a sample schedule. Figure 2.5 shows how that schedule might look in terms of percentages of time:

Figure 2.4 Elements of a Math Workshop

Component	Time Frame	Reason
Calendar	5–10 minutes	Everyday skills
Problem of the Day/ Number of the Day	5–10 minutes	Problem solving, mental math, ongoing skill practice
Whole-Class Mini-Lesson	10–12 minutes	Introduce or reinforce Big Ideas
Math Centers/Guided Math Group	12–15 minutes each (1–3 rotations)	Targeted interventions and purposeful practice
Math Strategy Practice/ Energizers	5–10 minutes	Fluency
Share/Class Journal/ Individual Journal	10 minutes	Summarize big ideas and reinforce mathematical takeaways

Figure 2.5 Workshop Time Frame

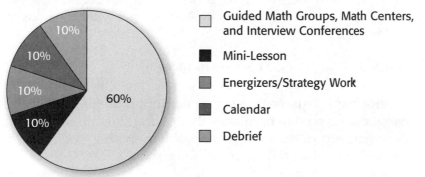

- Guided Math Groups, Math Centers, and Interview Conferences
- Mini-Lesson
- Energizers/Strategy Work
- Calendar
- Debrief

Guided math is a teaching structure that can be integrated into any existing math block. Although I prefer the math workshop model, if you are doing a traditional model, you can fit math workshop in by integrating it while the students work in their math journals. If you do a whole-group lesson and then have students work independently, during this time you could pull one or two groups for 10 or 12 minutes each.

The Math Workshop Schedule

Math workshop has several parts. Here is a picture walk through a regular day.

Calendar/Morning Routines (9:00–9:10)

Calendar work is really important in every grade. I am a big advocate of all students having their own calendars so they can practice things like writing numbers, filling in graphs, analyzing and discussing data, and tallying over time. All students should have their own calendar folder. The folders can be differentiated by levels with the novices having fewer pages than the practitioners. At the very least, the youngest children can fill in the day of the week, do the weather graph, do a tally chart, and count how many days they have been in school. In the upper elementary grades, students can note the weather in their calendar and talk about the fraction and/or percentage of days that it was sunny, rainy, or snowy.

Number of the Day

In Number of the Day activities, students take either the calendar day, the number of days they've been in school, or a random number and write about that number in a variety of ways. They talk about how to add and subtract numbers to make that number. They compare that number with other numbers. They show that number with base-ten blocks and write it in expanded form. They discuss whether it is odd or even, prime or composite. By working with the Number of the Day every day, they get on friendly terms with numbers (see Figure 2.6). So for instance, I might put the number 128 on the board and then write five things I want the class to do with it (see Figure 2.7).

Daily Word Problem/Vocabulary Review (9:10–9:20)

Writing is so important. I suggest that you model problems, do shared problem solving, do interactive problem solving, do think-alouds during the problem solving, and have students do problem solving in their journals. Model, model, model, and then model some more.

Figure 2.6 Number of the Day Posters

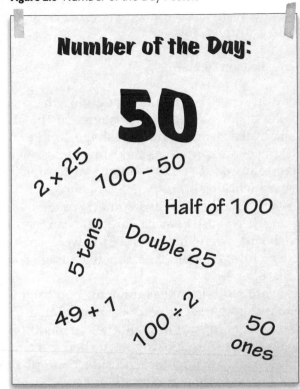

Figure 2.7 Number of the Day

Today's Number of the Day: 128

Spell it	Add 10	Add 1	Show it two ways in money	What comes next?
Show it in base ten	Subtract 10	Add 100	Subtract 100	Double it
Make a subtraction sentence in which this is the answer	Halve it	Round it to the nearest 10	Round it to the nearest 100	Add two or three numbers whose sum is 128

Be sure to do some type of review of math vocabulary every day. Make sure your math word walls *teach* the words! Always illustrate the words and provide lots of examples.

Whole-Class Mini-Lesson (9:20–9:30)

The class mini-lesson serves the purpose of giving the class a touchstone activity around the major concept. For instance, if the class is studying geometry, you might teach the students a shape song or an angle chant. If they are studying word problems, you might go over a word problem strategy chart to introduce a new strategy or reinforce something the whole class has been working on.

The mini-lesson usually employs some type of math artifact that records the thinking. If you use a smartboard, you can then save the lesson. If you use a whiteboard, you will then erase the work so there is no record unless you take a picture. I therefore usually encourage teachers to do the mini-lesson on chart paper.

If the students are studying measurement, you might read a picture book, play a whole-class game, or read a poem related to the topic. The idea of the mini-lesson is to start or continue a general discussion about the Big Ideas that students are looking at in their current unit of study. During your mini-lesson, you might teach a skill, concept, or strategy. Your mini-lesson should have some sort of math anchor chart so that students can reference it in the future.

Number Talks and Energizers

A number talk is a short talk about numbers. The focus is usually on strategies. This is sometimes done in small groups and sometimes as a whole class. For example, a number talk could be about all the different strategies to make ten. A number talk could also be about different ways to model a problem. For example, you might do a number talk around the addition problem $29 + 33$. Everyone would talk about ways to solve it and ways to model it. The students might even record their thinking in a notebook.

Math energizers are quick games that build fluency and automaticity (see Figure 2.8). Games like I'm Thinking of a Number are energizers because they get students thinking and talking about numbers in friendly ways. I play these games with the whole class as well as in guided math groups. They should take about five minutes. For example, in "I'm Thinking of a Number," the teacher thinks of a number and the students try to guess that number by asking questions. Is it more than or less than 15? Is it odd or even? Is it a two-digit number or a three-digit number? Through a series of questions, the students guess the number.

Figure 2.8 Tell Me All You Can Routine

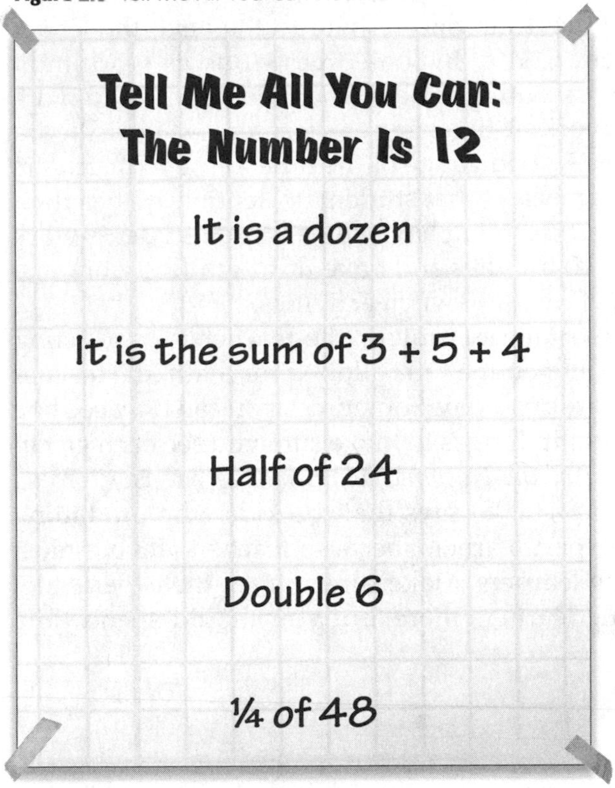

Tell Me All You Can: The Number Is 12

It is a dozen

It is the sum of 3 + 5 + 4

Half of 24

Double 6

¼ of 48

Here is an example of the game Tell Me All You Can. Sometimes students record the responses of the class and sometimes teachers record the responses.

First Rotation/Math Centers (9:30–9:43)

During this time the teacher pulls certain students into a small guided math group while the other students go to independent centers.

Student Math Centers
During the student activity period, a variety of things can happen. The students go to math centers and/or guided math groups. Sometimes, everyone is working at math centers because the teacher is doing math conferences and interviews with individual students. Students keep track of their work in centers by keeping a folder with artifacts of their center work. Students can go to a variety of centers, but many of the centers take place at their desks.

Often, centers are brought to students in bags or boxes by their group leader. I tend to have students stay at their tables to work in centers because I believe it saves instructional minutes. When students have to switch stations, they often waste time in the movement. I prefer to have the centers already prepared so the leader can bring two or three centers to the students. When it is time to switch from one activity to the next, the leader packs up Center A and opens Center B. Sometimes students work individually, sometimes they work with partners, and sometimes they work in groups. Students might work at the computer center, the smartboard center, or the big-book center. A good gauge of the time to spend in centers is the students' age. The research says that students' attention span is their age plus two or three minutes. So I might have kindergarten students work in one center between 7 and 10 minutes and have third-graders work at a center for 12 to 15 minutes before they switch activities.

While the students are working in centers, the teacher is conducting guided math groups. Depending on the time allotted for math, the teacher might see two or three math groups a day. Sometimes you can only see one math group a day. The important thing is to make sure you see each group every week. *The Final Report of the National Mathematics Advisory Panel* (U.S. Department of Education, 2008) says that the kids who are falling through the cracks are the expert learners, because teachers devote most of their time to the struggling learners. Make sure you see the experts too! You might see the struggling learners more, but you should spend time with the experts as well.

Big Switch (9:43–9:45)

The teacher gives some sort of signal and the students know to clean up their centers and get ready for their next station. I prefer chimes, a xylophone, or a song. Other teachers use bells, lights, or claps.

Second Rotation/Math Centers (9:45–9:57)

During this time the teacher pulls other students into a small guided math group while the rest of the students work at independent centers.

Share (10:05–10:15)

The share happens at the end of the workshop, when students share their thinking about the activities they have engaged in during the workshop. For example, if the students are working on comparing numbers and everyone has explored that topic in some form or another in their math centers at their level, the teacher might lead a discussion about "What's Important about Comparing Numbers." In this way, the teacher can concretize some of the enduring understandings. The teacher might keep a class journal of the discussions some days (see Figure 2.9). Other days, students might write in their "thinking notebooks" about their activities. The point of the

Figure 2.9 Math Class Journal Entry

February 17, 2012

Today in math class we worked on comparing numbers in our centers. Some people drew pictures to compare numbers. Some people compared numbers using the number line. Some people played the game High Number. In this game, they drew two cards and the person with the highest number wins both cards. The most important thing about comparing numbers is to look at the amount of both numbers. We used words and phrases like *greater than*, *less than*, *same as*, *more than*, and *fewer than*.

share is that students leave class with some specific takeaways about the Big Ideas of the unit.

Share time is also a time for students to sit in the Mathematician's Chair. This is similar to the Author's Chair in reading workshops. Students sign up to sit in the chair where they can share what they are learning, work that they did that day, or sometime during that unit. They lead a discussion about their work and they take questions. Oftentimes, the primary students use a toy microphone to talk. You can do this routine every day or once a week. You just fit it into the rhythm of your class.

It is very important to do this last part of the workshop. People tend to skip the share period. Never skip the share period. It is the part that brings closure to the math workshop. Just as you opened the workshop, you have to close up the workshop for the day. Otherwise the students are left to make meaning of the day on their own. The Share gives students some real clear takeaways for the day.

Summary

Guided math groups should take place within a mathematically rich environment. There are many components of a numerate environment that engage students in thinking flexibly about numbers, sharing their thinking out loud, and reflecting on their own learning. In math workshop, students have multiple encounters with math in various learning situations—individually, in partners, in groups, with the whole class. During math workshop, practice is distributed over time so students revisit skills in meaningful, engaging ways and learn to become confident mathematicians.

Reflection Questions

1. In what ways do you give students an opportunity to think flexibly about numbers throughout the year?
2. Do you use a variety of instructional strategies to launch discussions about your current unit of study? Which ones do you use? Do they tap into a variety of intelligences?
3. At the end of your math period, how do you summarize the learning? Do you ever write a class journal to document the key takeaways?

3

Managing the Math Workshop

Getting Started

Start slowly. Start calmly. Start immediately. Just start! The first few weeks are crucial. You should definitely take time to lay out the procedures and expectations for math workshop in general, and guided math in particular, so your students understand them from the beginning. If you don't use a workshop model, you still want to practice what guided math time looks like, sounds like, and feels like. You should be very explicit with your students about the procedures and the expectations. Students thrive in a predictable, well-managed, safe environment.

A word about pencils: We must spend 40 hours a year dealing with students' pencil problems (dull or broken tips, wanting to use the sharpener, running out of eraser, and so on). To solve all these problems ahead of time, just prepare a few hundred sharpened pencils at the start of the year.

Rules, Consequences, and Rewards

I recommend that you start the first week of school by getting your class to practice what to do. It is really important to spend the first few weeks of school establishing the rules, consequences, and rewards that will govern the rest of the year. Here are a few key things to remember. First, the *rules* should be clear, explicit, and few—perhaps three to five. According to classroom management theory, rules should be written in positive language, so no "Don'ts" or "Nevers." They should be written on a poster and hung on the wall and ideally established and agreed upon by the class as a whole. It's a good idea to get all the students to sign the rules, so they can't say later they didn't know. For example, three rules could be: 1) We respect each other, so we are kind in our words and actions; 2) We work hard all the time; and 3) We take care of our classroom materials.

Consequences should be immediate. There should be a sense of fairness: nobody should get more chances than anybody else. By chances I mean, for example, that students get a warning (you're on yellow) before they go directly to red. When students are off task in their centers, they should immediately be cautioned. When whole groups are off task, they should be required to put away their centers and go back to their desks. When there are immediate consequences, students learn fairly quickly to stay on task. They don't like sitting at their desks with nothing to do while everyone else is actively engaged.

All educators have their own philosophy on *rewards*. Some teachers believe in only intrinsic rewards while others believe in a balance between intrinsic and extrinsic rewards. Whatever your philosophy, don't bankrupt your economy. The bottom line is that your students get to keep the things they earn (whether that be pizza points, marbles, or tally marks). Taking away stuff that you already gave sends the wrong message—that what you have earned is not secure. So, if students have 50 points, you can't get mad and erase 10. That's not fair.

Establishing Routines

Students should understand the order of the day. They need to know exactly what to do during student activity time. They should be clear about their space and their activity. Basically, I tell them, there is a table leader for their center. The only person who can ever come to me is the table leader—and then only if there is an absolute emergency, like a fire! Students know that if there is a problem, they need to come to me only during the Big Switch and not while I am leading a group. We also make posters to remind students of their expected behavior.

Spend the first four weeks of school practicing the math workshop routines. First, teach the class the schedule. You want students to understand how the math block works. I would spend time just practicing the different components of math workshop—calendar, Number of the Day, mini-lesson, strategy practice, student activity, energizers, and share time. Students thrive on consistency and predictability, so your math time can flow like clockwork. I like to set timers so that we stick with the schedule. Sometimes I use noisy timers and sometimes I use quiet timers. There are even really cool ones, such as egg timers, sand timers, and alarm clocks, that you can pull up on interactive boards.

Second, teach the students what to do during student activity. You have to teach them to be independent. If you don't follow a workshop model, you need to get them to practice working in their workbooks on their own. If you do follow a workshop model (which I highly recommend), you teach them how to work in centers independently, with partners, and in groups. You also practice a variety of center activities.

People often ask what centers should be available in the beginning of the school year. I recommend that in the beginning the students review skills from the prior year and work in "hot topic centers." Hot topic centers include things that students always struggle with, like money, time, and basic facts. Students should practice games together as a class, with half the class representing one team and the other half representing the other team. You should never send students to a center that they have never seen before. Students should practice a concept in the guided-math group several times before you send them off to practice it on their own.

Third, you should spend time teaching students how to read task cards and how to transition from their desks to the computer station, the interactive board station, and the Big Book center station. They must practice doing individual work, playing games with partners and groups, and recording their thinking.

Finally, students need to practice basic classroom manners. You should fishbowl students (make a circle and have the students role play in the middle), playing with partners and in groups. Students can talk about what they saw that was really good behavior and what could change. They can chart what works when playing with partners and what works when playing with a group. They can role-play being a good group and being a group that is acting up. You want your students to see what they are talking about in action. They discuss what they should do, how they should treat each other, and what happens at the end of the game. Teaching students how to be good sports is important too! Actually, it is just as important to teach students how to act when they win as it is to teach them how to act when they lose!

Math Anchor Charts

During these first few weeks, you should spend time making classroom math anchor charts (see Figure 3.1, page 32). These posters highlight crucial math questions: What do good mathematicians do? How can students prove their thinking? What can students say when they are talking about math?

Students can also work on social skills posters, such as "What Is Sharing?" (see Figure 3.2, page 32) In the primary grades and English Language Learner (ELL) classrooms, there should be drawings or pictures to illustrate each section. Your students should work on a social skill until they learn it and then pick a new one.

Schedules

There are many different ways to make your schedule. You can write it on a whiteboard. You might write the entire schedule on the whiteboard, or you might write some of the schedule on the whiteboard and have the other half on cards stuck to the whiteboard (see Figure 3.3, page 33).

Figure 3.1 Math Anchor Charts

Math anchor charts are important because they give students visible reminders of the norms of the class, the work they are doing, different procedures, and content information.

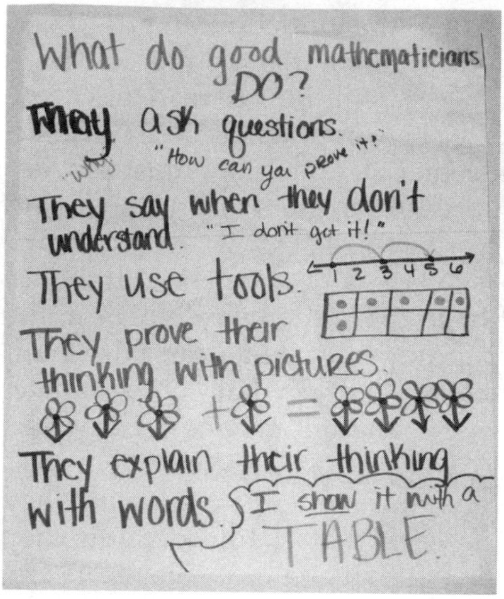

What do good mathematicians DO?

They ask questions.
"Why" "How can you prove it?"

They say when they don't understand. "I don't got it!"

They use tools.

They prove their thinking with pictures.

They explain their thinking with words. I show it with a TABLE.

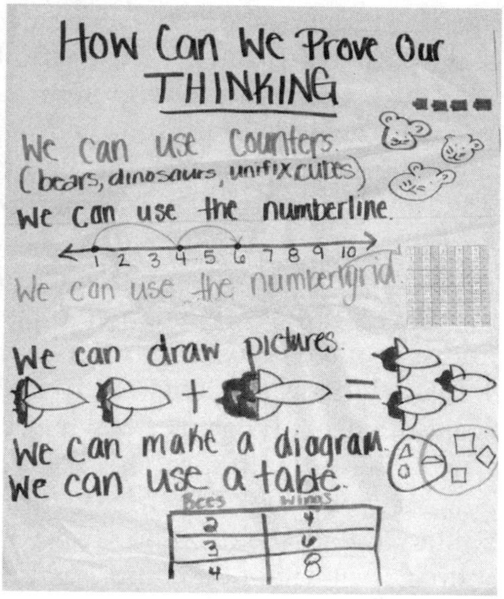

How Can We Prove Our THINKING

We can use counters. (bears, dinosaurs, unifix cubes)

We can use the numberline.

We can use the numbergrid.

We can draw pictures.

We can make a diagram.
We can use a table.

Figure 3.2 What Is Sharing?

Sharing Looks Like . . .	Sharing Sounds Like . . .	Sharing Feels Like . . .
Materials in the middle of the table Passing things to each other	"Please . . ." "Thank you" "May I . . ." "Can you wait . . ." "Yes, I can wait . . ."	Good Happy Great

Figure 3.3 Math Workstation Schedule

There are a variety of ways to record where students are going.

Math Workshop		
Group	**Round 1**	**Round 2**
Dolphins	Guided Math	Computers
Sea Otters	Computers	Guided Math
Whales	Word Problem Centers	Games
Star Fish	Games	Word Problem Centers

Word Problems	Games	Guided Math	Computers
Group 1	**Group 2**	**Group 3**	**Group 4**
Imani	Gabby	Debbie	Zack
Brittany	Marlon	Mark	Kelly
Maria	Jacob	Romel	Tisha
Lara	Bobby	Miguel	Jose
Elena	Michelle	Monique	Nicki

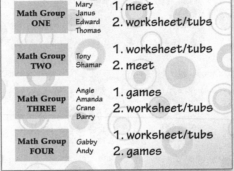

Math Group ONE	Mary Janus Edward Thomas	1. meet 2. worksheet/tubs
Math Group TWO	Tony Shamar	1. worksheet/tubs 2. meet
Math Group THREE	Angie Amanda Crane Barry	1. games 2. worksheet/tubs
Math Group FOUR	Gabby Andy	1. worksheet/tubs 2. games

Another option is to use sentence strip holders. Again, there are many different options. I really like to use the students' pictures. I also like icon cards so that there is a visual scaffold for students to read the math workshop schedule.

A third schedule option is using pocket charts with icons or pictures on each pocket. You can put the students' pictures on Popsicle sticks or you can put their names on sticks and put them in the pocket (see Figure 3.4, page 34).

Where Is the Guided Math Area in the Classroom?

Although there should be a specific area in the classroom where guided math groups are typically conducted, you can and should meet with your students in a variety of places. You should have a home base where most of your lessons, tools, and games are kept. Students need to be aware of that area and the routines surrounding it, such as coming to the area prepared, gaining access to the teacher during that time, and leaving the area.

Figure 3.4 Math Workstation Pocket Chart

Some people prefer to use pocket charts for their centers.

The guided math area should be set up with everything the teacher needs to conduct the lessons. The student folders, supplies, and math manipulatives should all be in organized and clearly labeled containers in the guided math area. This, obviously, involves much advanced planning and organization.

There are many places to operate a guided math group. Often students do meet their teacher at the kidney table. It's like home base. But other times you can meet your students in their math centers. You can hold your lessons at the interactive board or in the computer center as well. Or you can meet with the students on the floor in the meeting area. You meet wherever it makes sense.

Wherever the guided math group meets, you want to watch, ask questions, and take notes as your students play games and work on word problems. You might want to watch the students play a digital game or use virtual manipulatives to explain a topic. It is important to mix it up and do a variety of activities with the students. Sometimes students can focus on drawing, illustrating, and writing equations on the whiteboard. Other times, you'll want to use manipulatives.

Guided Math Teacher Toolkit

A teacher's guided math toolkit will help you keep all the things that you need to teach guided math lessons in one place (see Figures 3.5, 3.6, and 3.7, page 36). It should have folders for examples of student work that you want to keep, your anecdotal record-keeping charts, papers, pencils, and supplies. You should also have a supply container with dice, dominos, a deck of cards, and other manipulatives so that they are always ready to use. You should also have the supplies that the students need.

Staying organized is going to help you keep your sanity. There is so much going on in math workshop, you don't want to be running around looking for stuff that you need to do your lesson. Keep your stash stocked!

Figure 3.5 Tools for Guided Math

Sometimes I use the timer to time student activities.	In the guided math area, toolkits for each child should have an individual whiteboard.
Plastic plates make great whiteboards.	I often give pointers to students so they can point out the work they are doing.
Number lines are an essential part of a guided math toolkit. They can be used to add, subtract, multiply, divide, and do many other operations.	I use either store-bought erasers or socks as whiteboard erasers.

Figure 3.6 Writing Tablets

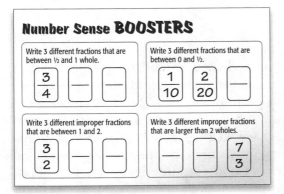

There are many different types of writing tablets that you can use in math class. You can decorate clear report folders with duct tape (preferably the fancy kind); these make great dry-erase mats. You can slip and slide different graphic organizers and work mats inside clear plastic folders and have students do some powerful work. You can also use white or colored plastic plates as whiteboards. They are fun and decorative. At teacher stores you can also buy clear mats to slip paper in and write on.

Figure 3.7 Teacher Toolkit

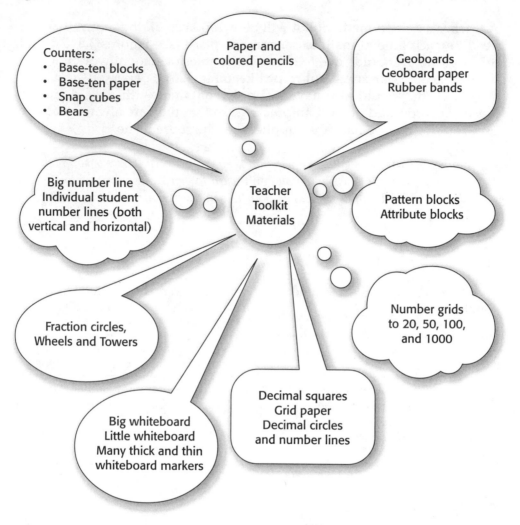

Counters:
- Base-ten blocks
- Base-ten paper
- Snap cubes
- Bears

Paper and colored pencils

Geoboards
Geoboard paper
Rubber bands

Big number line
Individual student
number lines (both
vertical and horizontal)

Teacher
Toolkit
Materials

Pattern blocks
Attribute blocks

Fraction circles,
Wheels and Towers

Number grids
to 20, 50, 100,
and 1000

Big whiteboard
Little whiteboard
Many thick and thin
whiteboard markers

Decimal squares
Grid paper
Decimal circles
and number lines

Summary

The key to guided math is getting a good start. Establishing expectations, including rules, procedures, rewards, consequences, and public protocols, makes the glue that holds the whole program together. Students work well when they know what to expect and when. They have to practice to get it right. Spending time in the first few weeks to establish your expectations for the class is far better than rushing into action and then having to correct your students' behavior all year long. Good planning is the key to a good program. If you plan, they will learn.

Reflection Questions

1. What types of public protocols do you use in your room now? What new ideas have you garnered from this discussion?
2. Do you have a teacher toolkit? Do your students have toolkits?
3. Do you explicitly work on social skills with your students? What do you think is the importance of teaching students how to get along with each other, and how do you think this learning can help your students to be well-rounded individuals?

4

Forming Guided
Math Groups

Working with Everyone

About a year ago, I was conducting a math interview with a first-grade boy named Miguel. We were going through the list of interview problems and question types and he was getting all the answers right. Finally, out of exasperation, he looked up at me and said, "Give me some hard ones!" I laughed, chucked the sheet, and started to make up harder problems. He was clearly bored with the current line of questioning. This happens so often in our classrooms. According to Lillian Katz (2000, p. 39), "when a teacher tries to teach something to the entire class at the same time, chances are, one-third of the kids already know it; one-third will get it; and the remaining third won't. So two-thirds of the children are wasting their time." Miguel seconds her point.

It is very important for teachers to work with small guided math groups at all levels, not just the lowest-performing. All students need the teacher's attention at some point to push them to the next skill level. Classroom assistants are a great help, but they should not be the only people who work with a particular group. By the end of every week, the teacher should have connected with every student in some form or another, possibly through small-group work, conferencing, or math interviews.

Forming Groups

In order to form effective guided math groups, teachers must first gather a variety of math data that gives a complete profile of each child. Before the beginning of a unit, a teacher might do pre-assessments that include surveys, quizzes, and/or mini-interviews. The teacher then plans for, implements, and evaluates guided math groups based on this data.

After this gathering of data, students are grouped into four main categories: (1) novice learners—those who do not have a basic understanding of the concept; (2) apprentice learners—those who have a basic understanding but need concentrated work to reach a deeper level; (3) practitioners—those who are working on grade level; and (4) expert learners—those who are working above the grade-level standard and need to have the topic extended. The teacher then works intensively with each group around specific content, strategies, and skills. Students need extensive practice with the content to gain proficiency. Ongoing classroom observations and quizzes provide the teacher with information about student progress.

The Role of Flexible Grouping

Guided math groups are organized according to the common needs of a specific group of students in a certain place and at a certain time. Here, it is important to make the distinction between traditional ability grouping and flexible groups. Ability groups have been a staple of education for a long time. Inevitably, students and everyone else know there is some sort of unnamed difference between the Bluebirds and the Sparrows. They tend to get different work, are treated differently, and ultimately feel different. (See Figure 4.1 for a detailed comparison between ability grouping and flexible grouping.)

Flexible grouping is completely distinctive. The teacher's goal is to engage in depth with groups of students around a particular instructional goal, with intensive practice. Guided math groups are flexible, meaning that they change over time. As students achieve particular knowledge and skills, the teacher moves the students to different groups.

Also, students can participate in different groups based on the content strand. For instance, Carlos is a smart geometrical thinker, but he does not have much facility with number facts. So Carlos is in the novice group for number facts but perhaps in the expert group during the geometry unit. This is why ongoing assessments are essential to the effective implementation of guided math groups. Through ongoing assessments, including quizzes, questionnaires, math running records, and anecdotal observations, teachers monitor and evaluate student progress. Teachers also schedule math conferences, in which students sit down and discuss their progress and plan for future work, as well as math interviews, during which teachers give oral assessments on particular skills.

Moreover, flexible grouping allows students to work together across groups, depending on what they are doing. For example, Carlos might work with a homogeneous group of expert-level learners during a skills lesson in geometry and then, when it is time to make shapes with Play-Doh for a center activity, he might be in a heterogeneous group. Flexible grouping

Figure 4.1 Comparing Ability Grouping and Flexible Grouping

Traditional Ability Math Grouping	Flexible Grouping
Children are grouped and labeled according to general achievement levels	Children are grouped according to specific needs based on the unit of study; there is a focus on strategy levels
Children work on concepts based on their level; low-level students get low-level work	Targeted interventions depend on the specific domain and standards; everybody gets challenging work at various levels of Bloom's taxonomy
Teacher sets the learning goals and purposes for math and predeter-mined concepts based on the math data	Teacher opens up a conversation and children talk about the math they are studying; they bring insights and make connections to their everyday lives
Groups are static	Groups are fluid
Different groups do different work	Everybody works on the Big Idea
Children rarely work with children outside of their group	Children work in a variety of groupings
Instruction is teacher-centered; teacher talks and students listen and then respond	Teacher coaches, facilitates conver-sation, leads discussion; students are active in the conversation
No writing is involved	Students write and share their thinking
Teacher gives standard end-of-chapter tests	Teacher uses a variety of assessments

Adapted from Opitz (1998).

allows Carlos to fluidly move in and out of a variety of groups depending on the particular focus of the activity.

Here are a few highlighted guided math schedules. In the first sched-ule (Figure 4.2, page 44), the teacher meets with one group a day. In the second example (Figure 4.3, page 44), the teacher meets with two groups a day, and in the third schedule (Figure 4.4, page 45) the teacher meets with three groups a day. How many groups you meet a day depends on your particular scheduling. There is no one right way to schedule. You have to pick a schedule that works for you and your students. You might, for example, meet groups just on Mondays and Wednesdays or Tuesdays and Thursdays.

Figure 4.2 Guided Math Weekly Schedule A

Guided Math Weekly Schedule
15-Minute Sessions—1 Session a Day

Monday	Tuesday	Wednesday	Thursday	Friday
9:30–9:45	9:30–9:45	9:30–9:45	9:30–9:45	9:30–9:45
Green Group	Blue Group	Green Group	Blue Group	Class Math Projects Podcasts/Videocast/ Glog/Photo Essay/ Class Mural/ Class Book

Figure 4.3 Guided Math Weekly Schedule B

Guided Math Weekly Schedule
15-Minute Sessions—2 Sessions a Day

Monday	Tuesday	Wednesday	Thursday	Friday
9:30–9:45	9:30–9:45	9:30–9:45	9:30–9:45	9:30–9:45
Green Group	Blue Group	Green Group	Blue Group	Class Math Projects Podcasts/Videocast/ Glog/Photo Essay/ Class Mural/ Class Book
9:45–10:00	9:45–10:00	9:45–10:00	9:45–10:00	9:45–10:00
Orange Group	Yellow Group	Orange Group	Yellow Group	Class Math Projects Podcasts/ Photo Essay/ Class Mural/ Class Book

Record Keeping

It's really important to have some sort of record-keeping system. You'll never remember which students you saw or what they did ten weeks ago if you don't have that information written down somewhere. Records of your work allow you to reflect on the past so you can analyze growth and plan for the future as well as make in-the-moment decisions. Record keeping also helps you facilitate discussions with your students about where they are in their math work, where they have been, and where they are going. If you are meeting with several groups a week and trying to successfully

Figure 4.4 Guided Math Weekly Schedule C

Guided Math Weekly Schedule
15-Minute Sessions—3 Sessions a Day

Monday	Tuesday	Wednesday	Thursday	Friday
9:30–9:45	9:30–9:45	9:30–9:45	9:30–9:45	9:30–9:45
Green Group	Blue Group	Green Group	Blue Group	Class Math Projects Podcasts/Videocast/ Glog/Photo Essay/ Class Mural/ Class Book
9:45–10:00	9:45–10:00	9:45–10:00	9:45–10:00	9:45–10:00
Orange Group	Yellow Group	Orange Group	Yellow Group	Class Math Projects Podcasts/ Photo Essay/ Class Mural/ Class Book
10:00–10:15	10:00–10:15	10:00–10:15	10:00–10:15	10:00–10:15
Purple Group	Pink Group	Purple Group	Pink Group	Class Math Projects Number Talks

juggle everything that goes along with that schedule, then you absolutely have to have some way of keeping track. Most importantly, your method of keeping track has to work for you. You should pick a system that you can really be accountable to. Figure 4.5 (page 46) shows some possibilities.

The Common Core State Standards (CCSS) for math have different strategy levels for the operations. You will want to keep track of your students' levels in some way. Figure 4.6 (page 46) provides an example. Figure 4.7 (page 47) shows a detailed guided math group planning sheet. In this particular example, the teacher is meeting with three groups a day.

Summary

Being organized is hard work for some of us. It takes time, energy, and patience. But there really is no alternative. You have to create a system that you *will use*. You have to commit to using it. You need to know who's on first, and how they are going to get to second, and how on earth everyone will make it to home base (grade level) by the end of the year.

Figure 4.5 Ways of Recording Student Work

Clipboard with Post-it Notes	Data Sheet	Waterfall Index Card Chart	Folder with Post-it Notes
Write each student's name on a Post-it note and stick them to a clipboard. During class, you can take brief notes under each name. This way, you can quickly see how many notes you have written for each student.	A specific observation protocol can be used. Use a clipboard to hold it and then, when done, keep it in a folder. Make several copies of the protocol and use as needed.	Take notes for each student on a large index card. By writing the students' names on the bottom of the cards, you can keep them all together, layered on a clipboard, and easily flip to individual students.	Keep Post-it notes in a manila folder with notes for each student. You can just keep adding notes on top of each other so you have all the notes on a single student in one place.

Figure 4.6 Guided Math Notes: Addition

Using Level 1 Strategies (counting out all of the items one by one and then adding them together)	Using Level 2 Strategies (counting on, drawing pictures)	Using Level 3 Strategies (using derived facts)
Taylor	Mary	Gabriel
Stephanie	Tom	Joseph
Lulu	Abigail	Zachariah
Harry	Marcus	Maria
	Malik	Kiyana
	Vanessa	
	Tiffany	
	Carlos	
	David	

Figure 4.7 Guided Math Planning Sheet

Date: _____

CCSS (Content Domain): Place Value

CCSS (Mathematical Practices): Math Talk (MP3) and Modeling (MP4)

Groups	Monday	Tuesday	Wednesday	Thursday
Group 1: Carla, David, Tom, Sheri, Tim	**GM: Using base-ten blocks to show two-digit numbers** Centers Centers	Centers Centers Centers	**GM: Two-digit Place Value Bingo** Centers Centers	Centers Centers Centers
Group 2: Stephen, Francisco, Maria, Terri, Trish	Centers **GM: Representing numbers with base-ten block drawings** Centers	Centers Centers Centers	Centers **GM: Two-digit Place Value Bingo** Centers	Centers Centers Centers
Group 3: Daniel, Mustafa, Kate, Mary, Scott	Centers Centers **GM: Using base-ten blocks to show two-digit numbers**	Centers Centers Centers	Centers Centers **GM: Two-digit Place Value Bingo**	Centers Centers Centers

Figure 4.7 Guided Math Planning Sheet *(continued)*

Groups	Monday	Tuesday	Wednesday	Thursday
Group 4: Tracie, Demorris, Kiyana, Shakhira	Centers Centers Centers	Centers Centers **GM: Using base-ten blocks to show three-digit numbers**	Centers Centers Centers	**GM: Three-digit Place Value Bingo** Centers Centers
Group 5: Kayla, Gary, Nicki, Bobbie, Tom	Centers Centers Centers	Centers **GM: Representing three-digit numbers with base-ten block drawings** Centers	Centers Centers Centers	**Centers GM: Three-digit Place Value Bingo** Centers
Group 6: Savannah, Robert, Frank, Bobbie, Gary	Centers Centers Centers	Centers Centers **GM: Discussing expanded form**	Centers Centers Centers	Centers Centers **GM: Three-and four-digit numbers**

Reflection Questions

1. How is your planning for guided math groups and centers? Is it explicit and written down somewhere or do you just do it mentally?
2. Do you know your students math strategy levels? What kind of records do you keep?
3. Do you ever meet with students in small groups? How fluid are those math groups?

5

Balanced Assessment: The Key to Grouping Students for Guided Math

About two years ago in my work as a math consultant, I was assessing a fourth grader on his multiplication tables. He was zooming through the interview when suddenly he came to a full stop at the beginning of the 12s. He took a long time before he tentatively started to say 24, 36, 48. I asked him what he was doing. He told me he was counting up. I was shocked. This guy could recite all the tables within a three-second time frame—except the 12s. So we started talking about strategies. I told him he could double the 6s, multiply the number by 10 and 2 and add those amounts together, or go up a set from the 11s. I also said he might think of other ways that would work. I stressed that although his strategy worked (if he didn't mess up somewhere along the way), it was quite slow and inefficient. Perhaps he might try another one. I agreed to meet him in a few weeks to see how his 12s were going.

I always remember this conversation because it reemphasized for me the importance of interviewing students. We absolutely do it in reading, but what happens with math? Why don't we think it's important to talk with students about their thinking and watch them do math out loud to see what strategies they are using? We need a big paradigm shift when it comes to assessing mathematical thinking and doing. We need a more balanced approach.

Balanced assessment means that we continually look at the whole student in a variety of ways. It means that we engage in ongoing assessment for learning and summative assessment of learning. We move beyond the paper-and-pencil math quiz and exam and move through a variety of ways to gather evidence of understanding. In classrooms where there is balanced assessment, students engage in a variety of pre-assessments, daily assessments, weekly ongoing assessments, and different types of evaluative assessments. Assessments are tools that allow us to collect evidence of understanding. We use different tools for different information. That is why it is very important to have a vast repertoire of assessments so we can know about the whole student. Throughout the different units of study, we want to have a systematic way of documenting information about students' learning.

Figure 5.1 How Do You Feel About Math?

Name: _____

Date: _____

1. Are you good in math?

2. Do you like math?

3. What are some things you remember about learning math in your other grades?

4. What is your favorite part about math?

5. Is there anything that you don't like about math?

6. Do you do math on your own when you don't have homework?

7. What do you want to learn in math class this year?

8. What do you do when you get stuck?

9. Do your friends like math?

10. Do the people you live with like math?

At the beginning of the school year, I give the students a variety of assessments to help me understand them in a holistic manner. For example, see Figure 5.1. I create a math profile for each of my students. My goal is to understand them as mathematical thinkers and to get a good idea of how proficient they are. So the series of assessments that I give them checks the five elements of mathematical proficiency: conceptual understanding, procedural fluency, strategic competence, adaptive reasoning, and mathematical disposition (see Figure 5.2).

Pre-Assessment for Forming Guided Math Groups

Pre-assessments are very important because they tell us where to begin. Often teachers just begin units without checking in with their class, having no idea where the students are starting from, only where they are

Figure 5.2 Questions About Mathematical Proficiency and Assessments to Collect Evidence

Element	Questions	Assessment Types
Conceptual understanding	Does the student understand this concept?	Math interview
Procedural fluency	Can the student do the math? Is she able to self-correct?	Math conference; entrance slip; exit slip; quiz
Strategic competence	Does the student have a variety of ways of thinking about this concept? Is he a flexible thinker? Does he use *different* strategies when solving problems? Does he use *efficient* strategies when solving problems?	Math interview; quiz; entrance slip; exit slip; math running record
Adaptive reasoning	Can the student talk about the concept? Can she explain it in her own words? Can she ask questions about it? Can she defend her thinking about it?	Entrance slip; exit slip; math interview
Mathematical disposition	What is the student's level of confidence when working with this concept? What does he do when he gets to something he doesn't know? Does he monitor his own learning? Is he able to reflect on what he knows and what he is still struggling with in a productive way? Does he view himself as a mathematician in general? Does he think he is good, bad, or just okay at math? Does he like doing math?	Math survey; questionnaire; math profile; checklist

© *Newton, 2013*

supposed to be. So, if the pacing calendar says page 91, the first question must always be, "Where are the students?" I remember being asked to come to a fifth-grade class and do a lesson on division. The teacher quickly handed me the Teacher's Guide and said the class was starting a new chapter on division. She opened the book to the page and sat the children on the rug. I smiled and set the book down and looked at the students.

I said, "Well, today we are going to start talking about division, but I know that you all have been in school for quite a few years now and I am

Figure 5.3 Division Survey

Name: _____

Grade: _____

Year: _____

1. When I hear the word *division*, I think . . .

2. Division is . . .

             easy   hard   in the middle

3. When it comes to division, I know . . .

             a lot   a little   some things

4. Here are some sample division problems:

5. Write a division word problem. Then solve it in one way and check it in another way.

6. Explain how to divide.

7. What is a remainder? Give two examples.

sure you have heard of division before. So, to start, I want to know what you all know about division. What is division? Who can give me some examples of when we use it? What are the tricky parts?" The students began to chatter about their ideas. I wrote them all down on a chart as they spoke. This was a type of whole-group pre-assessment that let me do a quick check on the temperature of the class as a whole.

I followed this up with an individual survey about division (see Figure 5.3).

The individual survey tells me what students think they know. It also allows me to check for mathematical proficiency because, as you may have noticed, the questions are designed around the five elements of proficiency. I check to see if the student has conceptual understanding, procedural fluency, strategic competence, and adaptive reasoning regarding division. I also check their disposition about division. All of these are important to tap into in your pre-assessments, ongoing assessments, and the summative assessment.

A follow-up written quiz shows me what the students actually do know. Often there is a discrepancy between what students think they know and what they actually know. So, for example, I'll ask students what they need to work on in multiplication. They will often name the usual suspects—the sixes, sevens, eights, and nines. But after I give them a written quiz, I find out they don't really know the threes or fours either. After they take the assessment, I have them reflect on how they did. Ongoing self-assessment is an essential part of data collection. The teacher shouldn't be the only one who knows what is going on. Students need to know where they are and where they need to be and what the plan is to get there.

I often give students a quick oral assessment as well. These can take as little as five minutes, or much longer if needed. I ask students a variety of questions, depending on what my focus is. Sometimes, I want to check for conceptual understanding, so I might ask a question like "Can you explain to me what a fraction is?" or "Why is ¼ smaller than ¾?" If I want to check for procedural fluency, I might ask them to explain how to multiply a one-digit number by a two-digit number. Often, when I am checking for procedural fluency, I will also be looking for strategic competence. I might ask, "What are two ways for me to add 8 + 9?" At other times, I ask students how competent they feel about doing a particular problem. I ask things like "Do you think multiplication is easy or hard? Why? What is the easiest part? What is the tricky part?" When I ask these types of questions, I am checking their mathematical disposition.

I think it is very important to use a variety of pre-assessments to understand what students know and do not know (see Figure 5.4, page 56). It is very important to do fact quizzes to see which sets of facts students know automatically and which ones they are struggling with and need to practice. For example, one group of students might be working on multiplication tables of twos, fours, and eights while another group is working on

Figure 5.4 Types of Pre-Assessment

Type	Reason to Use	Element of Mathematical Proficiency
Survey	Provides quick information about what students think they do and don't know and how they feel about this topic	Mathematical disposition
Checklist	Provides quick list of what students think they can and can't do	Mathematical disposition
Written quiz	Provides written evidence of what students can actually do	Procedural fluency; conceptual understanding; strategic competence; mathematical disposition; adaptive reasoning
Mini math interview	Gives insight into student's conceptual understanding, procedural fluency, strategic competence, problem-solving skills, and mathematical disposition	Procedural fluency; conceptual understanding; strategic competence; mathematical disposition; adaptive reasoning
Self-assessment	Offers student self-reflection based on data	Procedural fluency; conceptual understanding; strategic competence; mathematical disposition; adaptive reasoning
Running record	Provides quick information about strategic competence and procedural fluency	Procedural fluency

© Newton, 2013

threes, sixes, and nines. One way for students to identify and practice what they need to work on is to have a folder with two sides. One side is designated "Facts I know" and the other "Facts I need to know" so students can do targeted practice.

After I have gathered all this information, I use it for initial placement in the guided math groups (see Figure 5.5). For example, I organize all the information from the written quizzes and I divide the students into groups by levels. I like to keep the groups small, between three and five students,

Figure 5.5 Math Assessment Action Plan: Student Groups

Teacher: Newton   Grade: 4th

Date: 2/12   Big Idea: Shapes   Domain: Geometry   Unit: Chapter 7

Group Instructional Focus				
Drawing lines and line segments	Drawing lines and line segments	Angles	Angles	Classifying two-dimensional shapes based on line type
Kelly	Sean	Michael P.	Carlos	Tito
David	Stacy	Trevor	Marvin	Lela
Michael	Kiyana	Maria	Shakhira	Timothy

so I will often have more than one group per category. For example, during a multiplication unit, I might have two different novice groups and two different apprentice groups. The novices are working on facts 0 to 5. With this group, I still have to use a great deal of concrete materials and a variety of manipulatives to build conceptual understanding as well as procedural fluency. The apprentices are working on facts from 6 to 10. With this group, I use some manipulatives and a great deal of visuals. The experts who know all their single facts are working on single-digit by double-digit multiplication. I use manipulatives with them because I begin with an explanation using base-ten blocks. It is important to make an overall unit plan to see how all the pieces fit together (see Figure 5.6, page 58).

Ongoing Assessment

Ongoing assessment is crucial for guided math groups (see Figure 5.7, page 59). It helps you to know the effectiveness of the groups' work and the needs of the students. Since groups are flexible, students might move during the unit of study once they have mastered certain concepts, skills, and strategies. There are a variety of ways to keep track of students throughout the unit of study, including anecdotals, checklists, conferences, and running records.

Figure 5.6 Math Workshop Plans

	Week 1	Week 2	Week 3
Mini-lesson	**Big Idea:** Distributive property using the area model to explain multi-digit multiplication	**Big Idea:** Distributive property using the open array to model multiplication	**Big Idea:** There are a variety of strategies to solve multiplication problems
Guided math	**Skill Focus:** Using base-ten blocks to demonstrate area model of multiplication	**Skill Focus:** Using the open array to show multi-digit multiplication	**Skill Focus:** Using equations to show multi-digit multiplication
Math work stations	Using base-ten blocks to show multiplication	Using the open array to solve multiplication problems	Using general method and specialized strategies to multiply
Journal prompt	How does using base-ten blocks help us to show multiplication?	How does using the open array help us to show multiplication?	What are my favorite ways to do multiplication problems?

While I am working with students during the guided math session, I keep anecdotal notes of what is happening (see Figure 5.8, page 60). These notes help me to remember what happened and what's next. I write down what I see, what the students said, and what they did. Sometimes, I write down what they are saying to each other as they work together. Other times, I will ask specific questions and record the answers. Small-group work is the perfect time to push on mathematical thinking so that you can build adaptive reasoning.

Sometimes I walk around the room and make general observations of the work going on in different math centers. I write down what the students are doing, what they are saying, and any difficulties they seem to be having. I will engage students in group think-alouds. Sometimes, I just take notes. However, other times I walk around with a specific purpose. For example, I might be listening to the math talk that is taking place in the groups, using a specific protocol (Figure 5.9, page 61) to record the following information: (1) Which students are talking? (2) What are they saying? (3) Who is not talking? (4) Are they using math language? (5) Are they using the math artifact charts?

Figure 5.7 Types of Ongoing Assessment

Type	Reason to Use	Element of Mathematical Proficiency
Anecdotals	Provide a space to write down observations made during the math workshop	Procedural fluency; mathematical disposition; strategic competence; conceptual understanding; adaptive reasoning
Checklists	Provide a structure to make specific observations of behaviors, attitudes, and skills	Procedural fluency; strategic competence
Conferences	Provide different types of conferences to either reteach, assess, or celebrate	Procedural fluency; mathematical disposition; strategic competence; conceptual understanding; adaptive reasoning
Running records	Provide the opportunity to check fluency levels	Procedural fluency; strategic competence
Exit slips	Provide immediate feedback about what the student has just learned	Procedural fluency; mathematical disposition; strategic competence; conceptual understanding; adaptive reasoning

© *Newton, 2013*

I also use two kinds of writing graphic organizers to monitor student learning. I use one for myself (see Figure 5.10, page 62). Who is getting what we are doing? Who is struggling? What is the evidence? Do the students know where they are in the process? What types of self-reflections have we done so that everyone has an idea of where they are along the learning continuum? The second graphic organizer (Figure 5.11, page 62) allows students to check their own progress in the unit of study.

In teaching literacy, educators have a deep conviction that it is important to confer with students about their reading and writing. What we should know by now is that this is a structure that works in other curriculum areas as well. We have to start talking with students about their math. We have to ask questions, set goals, and have quick, deep discussions about learning. We must make it a point to confer with students at least twice a semester.

Figure 5.8 Anecdotal Notes

8/20 David Initial math interview: David is smart, quick, and energetic. He knows his facts and he wants to share what he knows. He can count to 100 and add and subtract through 10 mentally. He is using level 1 and level 2 strategies.
8/21 David Center work: David works well during center time. He stays engaged and plays well with his partner.
9/20 Guided math group David played a whole-group game today in guided math group. He did some powerful thinking. We were using ten-frames to make tens. He sees it and can explain it.
10/20 Whole-class discussion David shared his thinking today. He went to the whiteboard and drew a number line model for solving a word problem. It was organized and clear. Big smile at the end of sharing.
1/20 Mid-year Benchmark David did well on the mid-year assessment. He uses mainly level 2 strategies and some level 3. He had 90% correct on the test. The goal is to work on level 3 strategies now.

Figure 5.9 Teacher Observation Sheet

Date: _____ Activity: _____ Working with a partner Working with a group	What does the talk sound like?	Who is engaged?
Key words and phrases:	Who is talking?	Who is not talking?
What are they doing and how are they doing it?	What are the artifacts of the activity?	Other comments:

Evaluative Assessment

Evaluative assessment is necessary but not sufficient. Too often we give the end-of-chapter test and move on. We must use this information to make sure that all students are learning (see Figure 5.12, page 63). When we give a chapter test, we need to do an error analysis to see what types of mistakes and misconceptions our students still have. We then need to pull small groups and make sure those mistakes are corrected. It is not enough to know that six students missed the money problem. We need to

Figure 5.10 Teacher Check-In About Math Workshop

Date: _____   **Answer**

Have I set up scaffolded lessons for this unit?	
Have I set up tiered center activities?	
Have I given formative assessments this week?	
Do I know where all my students are in the learning process?	
What is the evidence of where my students are?	
Who is struggling and what am I doing to help them?	
Thoughts about this unit	

Figure 5.11 What Am I Learning?

1. Do I understand what we are learning?

2. How much?

        a little   a lot   somewhat

3. Things I would like to know more about:

Figure 5.12 Types of Summative Assessment

Type	Reason to Use	Element of Mathematical Proficiency
Chapter test	Provides a space to assess the learning of the current unit of study	Procedural fluency; strategic competence; conceptual understanding; adaptive reasoning
Self-reflection on chapter test	Provides an opportunity for students to self-assess their learning	Mathematical disposition
Math interview	Provides insight into how the student is thinking about the math and an opportunity to see what they are doing	Procedural fluency; mathematical disposition; strategic competence; conceptual understanding; adaptive reasoning
Performance assessments	Gives the students an opportunity to do the math instead of using paper and pencil: they work with manipulatives and tools to physically do something	Procedural fluency; mathematical disposition; strategic competence; conceptual understanding; adaptive reasoning

© *Newton, 2013*

find out what they did incorrectly. What are they thinking? What do they not understand? Then, how do we teach to correct that? Is it a conceptual misunderstanding or is it a procedural error?

After we analyze the tests, we need to go over the results with the class as a whole and with individual students. The class uses this opportunity to set goals. Students shouldn't be on a mystery train. If they know where they are going, they have a much better chance of getting there. So we have to talk with students about where they are and where they are going. Together, teachers and students must come up with a plan of how to get there. Too often in schools, teachers don't involve students in their own learning. Yet the research shows that when students are involved in their learning they do better.

In the upper elementary grades, I have started doing a post-test data check-in with students (Figure 5.13, page 64). This has proven very effective because students get to reflect on and talk about their misunderstandings. This talk takes place in small guided math groups and is key to correcting misunderstandings.

Math interviews are connected with this self-assessment. I often will interview the students who did poorly so we can discuss what happened

Figure 5.13 Student Reflection on Test

Name: _____   Date: _____

Test: _____   Class: _____

1. How did I do on this test?

2. What did I do well on?

3. What do I still need to practice?

4. What is my action plan for doing it?

© *Newton, 2013*

and where we need to go. To talk with students about what they have learned and have them express their understandings and the parts they might still be "fuzzy" about helps them to concretize their learning before they go on to the next concept.

Evaluative assessments should extend beyond the chapter and quarterly exams. At least twice a year, I like to give performance assessments in which students have to show me what they know by thinking through a real-life task with manipulatives. We do these by grade level as well so we can compare the data not only in the class but across the grade. There is an excellent website (see www.exemplars.com) for sample performance assessments.

Finally, we have to have somewhere to house all this information. I encourage teachers to use math data folders. Math data folders have sections for chapter quizzes, performance items, tests, teacher reflections, and student reflections. I firmly believe that data folders should be accessible to students and parents. The more people who know where we are going, the more likely it is we are going to get there. I also encourage teachers to use math portfolios for individual students in which, as the school year goes on, they can keep one thing from each unit of study that they think shows growth. Students should also select something from the unit of study that they would like to put in their portfolios. Sometimes teachers should offer a menu of choices from which students select what they want to go in their portfolio, write a small explanation of why they chose it, and explain how it represents their learning.

Summary

Balanced assessment is an integral part of planning and successfully implementing guided math groups. Pre-assessment helps to determine students' particular needs. Strategic ongoing assessments give feedback to the teacher about what students are learning and what they are struggling with. Evaluative assessments are another link in the evidence chain that guides further instruction.

Reflection Questions

1. What types of pre-assessments do you use? What new ideas have you gathered from this chapter?
2. What types of ongoing assessments do you use? What new ideas have you gathered from this chapter?
3. What types of summative assessments do you use? What new ideas have you gathered from this chapter?
4. What is your overall balanced assessment plan?

6

A Framework
for Guided Math Lessons

Before the Lesson

Planning is the key to making the most of guided math lessons. The teacher must be sure to collect different data to decide what the point of intervention is. This data includes oral assessments, teacher observations, quizzes, tests, interviews, and conference notes. Based on the specific intervention and the plan of action, it is imperative to have all the necessary materials in the Teacher's Toolkit to teach the concepts and skills.

After collecting the data, the teacher must analyze, interpret, and decide on a plan of action. This is crucial. For instance, you might look at the math test data and decide that a certain group of children missed a certain type of question about patterns. Perhaps the students can identify patterns and extend them but have trouble describing them in written form. So you might then pull a guided math group based on this data and work intensively on this particular concept with those children. You make a plan, selecting a teaching activity that is at the instructional level of the children. For instance, you might plan to meet with this particular group three times and to present the information three different ways.

The first meeting might focus on using manipulatives and building understanding at the concrete level. The second meeting might focus on using pictorial representations. The third meeting might focus on teaching the concept at the abstract level. You also write in your plan that you will create follow-up work for the center activities as well as include extra homework with a note to the caretakers about these students' difficulty with this topic. The groups are flexible and based on the needs that the data shows. After you've done this planning, you are ready to meet with the group.

An Overview of the Framework for Guided Math Lessons

There is a specific framework for doing guided math lessons. This framework differentiates the work from just pulling students together in a small group. During a guided math lesson, the teacher (1) presents a brief mini-lesson based on a concept, strategy, or skill highlighted in the data gathered about the students; (2) presents a focus for the meeting; (3) outlines learning expectations; (4) models or demonstrates the math concept, strategy, or skill; (5) gives the children the opportunity to discuss and practice the math; (6) monitors the children as they practice, taking notes and asking probing questions; (7) brings the group back together for a debrief, reemphasizing the major teaching point, making any necessary clarification, and soliciting further questions or comments; and (8) finally discusses next steps, such as practice in the math centers and homework.

There are many different types of guided math lessons that you can give (see Figure 6.1). You might teach a concept. You might play a game with the students on the computer. You might conduct a word-problem-solving session in which students tell, listen to, and solve each other's word problems using ten-frames, rekenreks, and other tools. You might have the students record their thinking on artifact sheets, such as Venn diagrams, Frayer models, and game recording sheets.

Presenting the Mini-Lesson

During the first part of the guided math session, the teacher must hook the students into the lesson. Do this by making some sort of connection to past lessons, present conversations, or future endeavors. You then clearly explain the focus of the lesson, presenting specific learning expectations. The teaching point can be a concept, strategy, or skill.

You then model and/or demonstrate the student activity, checking for understanding throughout the process. So, for instance, you might model a way to describe patterns. You might then practice this method with the small group.

Student Practice

After the teacher's demonstration and checking for understanding, the students then practice this skill on their own and take turns describing their individual patterns to the group. This period has often been called active engagement (Calkins, 2001; Collins, 2004), when much scaffolded discussion takes place. You give and elicit feedback from the students in the group. You ask very specific types of questions to facilitate the students' mathematical thinking. During this stage of the lesson, you interact with the students while they are doing the math, scaffold the work, and provide interventions. You might also be taking anecdotal notes and writing notes in your guided math practice log.

Figure 6.1 Games in Guided Math Lessons

Lesson Type	Example
Games One helpful thing to do in a guided math group is to play a game to practice a skill.	Kazam! is a great game for practicing counting money. You glue different coins to popsicle sticks. The sticks go in a cup with the handles poking up. You also add some "Kazam sticks" with amounts to subtract or add. To practice counting money, students pick a stick and add up the coins. They get to keep the totals as points, but if they pick a Kazam stick, they could either earn points or lose points, depending on what the stick says.
Working with Manipulatives Another way to do a guided math lesson is to have students work on modeling math problems.	Do a mini-lesson on how to model addition sentences with counters. Then give the students a set of problems to model. Watch to see what students do, ask questions, give clues, and listen to students explain their thinking.

Share Time

After the children have had ample time to practice, you will bring them back together for a debrief of the lesson. You ask probing questions about the math that they did. You also ask individual children to summarize the

Figure 6.2 Guided Math Planning Sheet

1. First, introduce the concept, skill, or strategy. Use questions to tap into children's prior knowledge about the topic and help them make connections between the topic and what they already know.
    *   Hook students.
    *   Emphasize vocabulary.
    *   Take comments.
    *   Ask questions.
2. Set the focus for the meeting.
    *   "Today we will . . ."
3. Outline learning expectations.
    *   "You will learn how to..."
    *   "You will be practicing . . ."
4. Model; check for understanding.
5. Discuss and do the math.
    *   Have students do guided practice together with the group, with a partner, or alone.
6. Monitor student work.
    *   Listen to students' conversation.
    *   Watch students work (let your observations guide your next moves).
7. Debrief: Summarize major takeaways; highlight main points; discuss tricky parts.
8. Discuss future plans.

focus of the lesson. Before the lesson closes, you review the teaching points and ask if anyone is still confused or has any general comments. You then give the students directions about the math center work (if centers are being used), which will reinforce what the class has been doing, as well as any follow-up homework that gives children a chance to practice the math. It is a good idea to write out the plan of action using some type of planning sheet (see Figure 6.2).

A Guided Math Lesson in Action

Let's take a look at a guided math lesson in action. The left column of Figure 6.3 lists the actual elements of the lesson. The right side is the scenario of a guided math lesson in action.

Figure 6.3 Guided Math Intervention Lesson 1

Ms. Leon has just finished analyzing the Chapter 3 math test in her third-grade classroom. She noticed that a few children had trouble counting money. She has decided to group these children together for a series of three guided math intervention lessons to build their skills. These students were labeled apprentices because they got some of the money problems correct and some of the money problems wrong on the test. Ms. Leon has called the children to the table in the back of the classroom where guided math lessons are held. She has set out a bag of coins, a workmat, and a worksheet for each student.

Mini-lesson	Ms. Leon: Hello, everyone. Today I have called you all together because, based on the math test, it looks like you all need to practice counting
Connection to real life; establishing relevance	money. Why do you think I want you to learn how to count money?
	Kyle: Because money is important!
	Ms. Leon: How so? Why do we need to know how to count it? When do we count it?
	Tara: We count it all the time. We count our lunch money. We count at the store.
	Kyle: We just counted it at the book fair!
Clear purpose	Ms. Leon: That's right. We use money often in our daily lives. So first I want you to know how to count money because you need to know how
Involving student in lesson	to count it right so you don't get ripped off. Second, I also want you to know how to count money because it is going to be on the state test in March. That is for sure. There always are some money problems on the third-grade test. So today we will practice counting money. But
Getting students to self-monitor their learning	before we start, I have a question. What do you all find as the tricky part?
Teaching point 1	Kala: Knowing where to start. I get confused.
	Tom: Me, too . . . I just mess up.
	Ms. Leon: Okay. When we count money, first we should sort it by like coins. Who can tell me what that means?

Figure 6.3 Guided Math Intervention Lesson 1 *(continued)*

Using wait time and encouraging thinking

John: It means put all the pennies together, then all the nickels, then all the dimes . . . like that.

Checking for understanding

Ms. Leon: Yep, that's right. So first we have to sort the coins. Then who can tell me what we might do next. [Silence . . . waiting] Oh, surely somebody has an idea! Who wants to give it a try and explain what we would do next to count the money.

Tom: Well, we count the big ones first.

Ms. Leon: What do you mean by the big ones? Are you talking about size?

Tom: Yes, you know, first the quarters, then the dimes . . .

Ms. Leon: Oh, so you are talking about the value . . . how much it is worth . . . not the size of the coin. . . .

Tom: Yeah.

Revoicing; focusing on teaching points

Ms. Leon demonstrates an example and then does two more with the group. She has scaffolded the activity so that the students start with easy problems and move on to work with harder examples later. Also note that Ms. Leon believes in ongoing test preparation embedded throughout the curriculum during the year, as opposed to a separate program usually done in isolation, not connected with the present learning, and more often than not taught in several consecutive weeks before the test. So Ms. Leon presents the problems to the students now, during the present unit of study, in the way that they appear on the state test.

Ms. Leon: Okay then, John has talked about first sorting it by coins—putting all the like coins together—and then Tom has talked about counting them, starting with the highest values. Let's try an example from the worksheet. "Cliff has these coins. [Coins are shown in mixed-up order on the page]. How much money does he have in total?" What should we do first?

John: Sort the money. There are two quarters, a dime, a nickel, and a penny. So the two quarters make 50 cents and 10 more cents would be 60 cents and then a nickel would be—

Kala: 65 cents—

Tom: And one more penny would be 66 cents.

Figure 6.3 Guided Math Intervention Lesson 1 *(continued)*

Eliciting agreement or disagreement	Ms. Leon: Okay, everybody look at the problem again and show me with a hand vote if you agree that 66 cents is the answer—thumbs up for yes, down for no, and sideways for maybe. Okay, you're all right! Great, let's try another one.
	Ms. Leon: Okay, who can tell me what we practiced today?
As the children work through two more problems as a group and then two problems on their own, Ms. Leon reiterates the strategy for counting coins, asks questions, and takes some notes in her guided math log.	Kyle: Counting money. Ms. Leon: What strategy did we focus on? Tom: Sorting and counting up.
Debrief includes a summary, further questions for clarification, and a final checking of understanding.	Ms. Leon: Okay, so who can summarize what we did today? John: We practiced counting money by sorting it and then counting up from the biggest coin.
Checking for understanding and having children restate a group member's point	Ms. Leon: One more question just to make sure we all agree: What does John mean by the biggest coin? Is he talking about size or value—that is, how much it is worth? Tom: He is talking about value.
Instructions about follow-up activities. After the students have left, Ms. Leon writes some final notes and future plans in her guided math log.	Ms. Leon: Now, when you go back to your centers, you will be practicing counting money. I have put some coin puzzles in your center container. Also in your homework packet I put some sheets so you could practice. Any questions, comments, or concerns? Tom: Can I go to the bathroom?

* Note that many of the teacher moves are talk moves discussed in Chapin, O'Connor & Anderson, 2009.

Evaluating Guided Math Lessons

It is really important to reflect along the way. The teacher should be taking anecdotals, making observations, questioning students, and watching the math in action during the guided math lesson. The teacher should be reflecting on the level of student engagement: (1) Are the students picking up and independently applying the concepts, strategies, and skills discussed? (2) Does this carry over into independent work? (3) Are students developing fluency with basic facts and flexibility with numbers and their thinking skills? (4) Can students talk about and model their mathematical thinking?

Summary

Guided math lessons follow a particular protocol. You don't just pull some students together and work with them randomly. It involves an explicit introduction, student work time, and a targeted debrief. There are many different types of planning templates (see Figures 6.4 and 6.5, page 80, for more ideas). A guided math session is a special interaction between the students and the teacher. Each party plays a particular role (see Figure 6.6, page 81). It is about getting students to talk, show their work, and name the strategies they are using.

Reflection Questions

1. What are the benefits of using manipulatives during guided math groups?
2. Do you consider how to teach a specific topic at the concrete, pictorial, and *then* abstract level?
3. Do you always make the math clear to the students? Do you begin the lesson by telling them what you are going to talk about and end it by summarizing what the class has done for the day?
4. How often do you play games in your guided math group lessons?

Figure 6.4 Guided Math Planning Template

Guided Math Planning Template

Teacher: _____   Big Idea: _____

Class: _____

Enduring Understandings: _____

Unit of Study: _____   CCSS Content Domain: _____

Monday		
Group: _____ Big Idea: _____ ____ Concept building ____ Procedural fluency ____ Strategy work ____ Reasoning ____ Problem solving ____ Talking about math ____ Using tools ____ Modeling Materials: _____	Group: _____ Big Idea: _____ ____ Concept building ____ Procedural fluency ____ Strategy work ____ Reasoning ____ Problem solving ____ Talking about math ____ Using tools ____ Modeling Materials: _____	Group: _____ Big Idea: _____ ____ Concept building ____ Procedural fluency ____ Strategy work ____ Reasoning ____ Problem solving ____ Talking about math ____ Using tools ____ Modeling Materials: _____
Vocabulary:		

Figure 6.4 Guided Math Planning Template *(continued)*

Tuesday		
Group: _____	Group: _____	Group: _____
Big Idea: _____	Big Idea: _____	Big Idea: _____
____ Concept building ____ Procedural fluency ____ Strategy work ____ Reasoning ____ Problem solving ____ Talking about math ____ Using tools ____ Modeling	____ Concept building ____ Procedural fluency ____ Strategy work ____ Reasoning ____ Problem solving ____ Talking about math ____ Using tools ____ Modeling	____ Concept building ____ Procedural fluency ____ Strategy work ____ Reasoning ____ Problem solving ____ Talking about math ____ Using tools ____ Modeling
Materials: _____	Materials: _____	Materials: _____

Materials:

Wednesday		
Group: _____	Group: _____	Group: _____
Big Idea: _____	Big Idea: _____	Big Idea: _____
____ Concept building ____ Procedural fluency ____ Strategy work ____ Reasoning ____ Problem solving ____ Talking about math ____ Using tools ____ Modeling	____ Concept building ____ Procedural fluency ____ Strategy work ____ Reasoning ____ Problem solving ____ Talking about math ____ Using tools ____ Modeling	____ Concept building ____ Procedural fluency ____ Strategy work ____ Reasoning ____ Problem solving ____ Talking about math ____ Using tools ____ Modeling
Materials: _____	Materials: _____	Materials: _____

Workstations:

Figure 6.4 Guided Math Planning Template *(continued)*

Thursday		
Group: _____	Group: _____	Group: _____
Big Idea: _____	Big Idea: _____	Big Idea: _____
____ Concept building ____ Procedural fluency ____ Strategy work ____ Reasoning ____ Problem solving ____ Talking about math ____ Using tools ____ Modeling	____ Concept building ____ Procedural fluency ____ Strategy work ____ Reasoning ____ Problem solving ____ Talking about math ____ Using tools ____ Modeling	____ Concept building ____ Procedural fluency ____ Strategy work ____ Reasoning ____ Problem solving ____ Talking about math ____ Using tools ____ Modeling
Materials: _____	Materials: _____	Materials: _____

Workstations:

Students		
Group 1	Group 3	Group 5
Group 2	Group 4	Group 6

Reminders:

Figure 6.5 Guided Math Group Planning Sheet

Level: Novice   Apprentice   Practitioner   Expert

Big Idea: _____

CCSS Standard: _____

CCSS Mathematical Practices: _____

Title of Lesson 1

Title of Lesson 2

Materials:

Questions: Additional Notes:

Figure 6.6 Roles and Responsibilities During Guided Math Group Instruction

Teacher	
Engage in ongoing assessment *Keep detailed records of what has been taught and next steps*	
Before the lesson	• Form groups based on current, relevant math data and differentiated instructional needs • Plan the mini-lesson, student activity, and focused share for the lesson, anticipating possible misunderstandings; also plan questions throughout • Prepare manipulatives, games, scaffolded activity sheets ("just right" concepts, strategies, and skills to guide students to becoming proficient mathematicians)
Intro (mini-lesson)	• Set focus for lesson: explain the mathematical goals for the lesson in clear language • Go over any relevant vocabulary or sentence structures • Model the concept, strategy, or skill • Make connections to real life
During (work period)	• Watch the students "do the math" • Listen intently to students' conversation • Observe and record students' strategies and their talk throughout the process • Support, prompt, and question • Acknowledge students' efforts • Interact with children throughout work period • Continually check for understanding through questioning strategies • Assist when appropriate
After (debrief)	• Lead share • Ask focus questions • Concretize learning by reviewing the specific math focus of the lesson • Facilitate conversation through various questions • Check in with individual students about their daily learning • Prepare students for follow-up work at math centers

Student	
Intro (mini-lesson)	• Listen, talk, question • Participate in discussion when asked by teacher to clarify, question, rephrase, give examples
During (work period)	• Participate in discussion with classmates and teacher • Interact with partner • Do independent work as assigned • Ask for help or clarification when needed • Try different strategies • Keep trying and don't give up
After (debrief)	• Talk about math work done during lesson • Check work • Reflect on own understanding • Do follow-up work at math center and for homework

7

Building Mathematical Proficiency in Guided Math Groups

I've been teaching for more than 20 years. But about nine years ago, when I first started doing math consulting, I was reminded of some very important things. I was coaching a new teacher of a fifth-grade class in the South Bronx. One girl was being extraordinarily rowdy and disruptive, so I pulled her out of class. As soon as we got outside the room, she propped herself up against the wall and proclaimed how much she hated math.

Unsurprised, I asked her what she wanted to be when she grew up. She quickly said she wanted to be a singer. I said that that was fantastic but that she would absolutely need to know some math to do that. She looked at me quizzically and said, "Never. I'll hire people." I said, "But you need to know for yourself how much money they owe you. What percentage you'll get from selling so many records." She retorted smugly, "I'll hire people." I insisted, "They steal. Don't you watch MTV and VH1? All kinds of singers get their money stolen by the people they hire." She smiled and responded, "I'll get the police to get them." I lowered my voice and whispered, "They go to Brazil. Nobody catches them in Brazil."

She looked appalled. I frowned at her and emphasized that she might want to learn some math for her career's sake. She finally agreed that it might be a good idea. Then she confessed, "Don't you tell anyone—I don't know how to multiply." Here we were doing 34 × 456 and she didn't even know what 3 × 4 was.

Then I remembered that students act up when they don't understand. It's easier that way. If they succeed in getting kicked out of class, then they don't have to do the work that they can't do. So I looked at her, deep into her soul, and I promised her that I would teach her how to multiply. That year, I pulled several small guided math groups and taught her and her buddies how to multiply, from the beginning. It was a watershed for all of us. I realized more than ever that teachers have to meet students exactly where they are and take them where they need to be. Those students finally realized they could learn math. It was a win-win.

I was reminded that being mathematically proficient is way more than just knowing how to do something. It is an attitude, a way of thinking, a style of engagement mixed in with understanding and knowing how to do stuff.

Guided math groups provide an up-close opportunity to build mathematical proficiency. The research defines it as having five components: (1) conceptual understanding, (2) procedural fluency, (3) strategic competence, (4) adaptive reasoning, and (5) mathematical disposition (National Research Council, 2001).

Conceptual Understanding

Students with conceptual understanding know what they are doing on a conceptual level. Often when we pull guided math groups, we first teach the concept. This requires that we have a toolkit available with different manipulatives, scaffolds, and tools. For example, a teacher who wants to teach the concept of dividing decimals might use money to get students to make connections with decimals in real life. Let's take a look at a lesson.

> **Teacher:** Hello everyone. Today we are going to look at what it means to divide decimals. We are going to be using money because this is where we divide decimals every day. Here is 28 cents [teacher shows 28 pennies]. As you already know, it is also known as 28 hundredths. Say you're going to give this money to four friends. How much money does each friend get? Who has a way we can figure that out?
>
> **Timmy:** We could just make four groups and put an equal amount in each group.
>
> **Teacher:** Okay, sounds like a plan. Use your workmat and show us how you would do that.
>
> **Timmy:** [draws four circles on his workmat and divides the coins into 4 equal groups] I got 7 cents in each group.
>
> **Teacher:** Okay, so does that make sense?
>
> **Sheila:** Yes, it is a fair share.
>
> **Teacher:** So what would be the answer?
>
> **Timmy:** .28/4 equals .07.
>
> **Teacher:** Okay, let's try another one. What's .30 divided by 5?

The students continue with this model, working together at first and then eventually working with a partner to solve some problems that they pulled on cards. Finally the teacher brings them back together for a debrief of the lesson.

Figure 7.1 Conceptual Understanding in the Common Core State Standards

Content Domain: Number & Operations in Base Ten

Kindergarten	K.NBT.A.1: Compose and decompose numbers from 11 to 19 into ten ones and some further ones
Grade 1	1.NBT.B.2: Understand that the two digits of a two-digit number represent amounts of tens and ones
Grade 2	2.NBT.A1: Understand that the three digits of a three-digit number represent amounts of hundreds, tens, and ones
Grade 3	3.NBT.A.1: Use place value understanding to round whole numbers to the nearest 10 or 100
Grade 4	4.NBT.A.1: Recognize that in a multi-digit whole number, a digit in one place represents ten times what it represents in the place to its right
Grade 5	5.NBT.B7: Add, subtract, multiply, and divide decimals to hundredths

© *2010 Common Core State Standards Initiative*

The new Common Core State Standards for math place a big emphasis on building conceptual understanding. There are several places across the domains where students work on knowing what a concept means rather than just knowing how to do something. Students are expected to explain and illustrate their understanding of concepts. Figure 7.1 is a chart that shows just some of the content domains and grade levels that require conceptual understanding.

Procedural Fluency

Procedural fluency is another component of mathematical proficiency. Procedural fluency deals with understanding how to do mathematical procedures. It "refers to knowledge of procedures, knowledge of when and how to use them appropriately, and skill in performing them flexibly, accurately and efficiently" (National Research Council, 2001, p. 121). Once students have conceptual understanding, they need to know how to actually do the math. Students also need to use that conceptual understanding to compute flexibly using different methods. The National Research Council (2001, p. 121) states that these methods include "written procedures, mental methods for finding certain sums, differences, products or quotients, as well as methods that use calculators, computers, or manipulative materials." So we

Figure 7.2 Guided Math Lesson on Procedural Fluency

Lucky 8

Lucky 8
You're so great
When I see you
I know what to do
Go to the other number
And take two!

Mrs. Rodriguez: Hi, everyone. Today we are going to practice how to solve Lucky 8 and Lucky 9 problems. Do you guys remember our poem? Let's see how we can use it to help us add fast. Let's say I had $98 + $57. When I look at this problem, I think I'll start with 98. I'm going to take 2 from the 57 and make that 98 a 100. Then, I'll add 100 + 55. Does that make sense? Can I do that?

Kayla: Yes, we did that when we were adding just 8s.

Timothy: Yes, it makes adding fast.

Mrs. Rodriguez: Okay, who wants to try the next one?

Kayla: I do. It's easy.

Mrs. Rodriguez: Let's say we had 78 + 44. What's the first thing you should do?

Kayla: I should make the 78 an 80. I have to take 2 from 44. That makes 42. Then I add 80 + 42.

Mrs. Rodriguez: What is a fast way to add that?

Michel: You could make 42 into 20 + 22 and then add 80 + 20 to get 100. Then you could add 22.

Mrs. Rodriguez: Okay, so let's look at another problem. What about 48 + 133?

Maria: Well, first make the 48 a 50. That leaves 131. Then I would just start with 131 and add 50, which makes 181.

Mrs. Rodriguez: Okay, I am going to give you guys some Lucky 8 flash cards and you will play with a partner. I am going to listen into your conversations as you explain your strategies to each other. I am going to give each one of you a different problem and I want you to work it out and be ready to explain what you did. [passes out differentiated problems, specifically chosen to help students think about using strategies such as landmark numbers, friendly tens, and compensation: 59 + 65, 38 + 77, 288 + 49, 123 + 498. The children work on the problems and then take turns

---

see procedural fluency requirements across the content domains as well. Figure 7.2 is a sample guided math lesson on procedural fluency.

The new Common Core State Standards for math stress the important relationship between conceptual understanding and procedural fluency. There are several places across the domains where students work on procedures based in conceptual understanding. Figure 7.3 is a chart that shows just some of the content domains and grade levels that require procedural fluency.

Figure 7.2 Guided Math Lesson on Procedural Fluency *(continued)*

showing and explaining their work.] Okay, now that we have practiced some, who can talk about the importance of this strategy?

David: It helps to play with the numbers and do it fast ways.

Mrs. Rodriguez: [allows students to work for a few minutes and then pulls them back together] All right, who can tell me what we were working on today in our guided math group?

Maria: We were working on adding fast with Lucky 8.

Mrs. Rodriguez: Who can add to that? What does it mean to use Lucky 8?

Timothy: It means when you see an 8 you can take 2 from the other number so you have a friendly number to add. Tens are our friends. You find a 10 and you can go faster.

Mrs. Rodriguez: Okay, so we will continue looking at this strategy along with some others. We are going to be looking at Lucky 9 next time. In your centers, you guys are going to be practicing working with Lucky 8 like we did in the group here today and also do a few practice problems for homework. Any questions or comments? Okay, if not then you can go get started.

Figure 7.3 Procedural Fluency in the Common Core State Standards

Content Domain: Operations & Algebraic Thinking

Kindergarten	K.OA.A.5: Fluently add and subtract within 5
Grade 1	1.OA.C.6: Add and subtract within 20, demonstrating fluency for addition and subtraction within 10
Grade 2	2.OA.B.2: Fluently add and subtract within 20 using mental strategies
Grade 3	3.OA.C.7: Fluently multiply and divide within 100
Grade 4	4.OA.C.5: Generate a number or shape pattern that follows a given rule
Grade 5	5.OA.B.3: Generate two numerical patterns using two given rules

© 2010 Common Core State Standards Initiative

Strategic Competence

Strategic competence is about students being able to solve problems and represent their thinking. The National Research Council (2001, p. 124) report defines it as "the ability to formulate mathematical problems, represent them and solve them." There is an emphasis on students representing their thinking about the math, either "numerically, symbolically, verbally or graphically." Strategic competence stresses that students don't just go straight for the answer but rather look for a "pathway" to find the solution; indeed, they actually avoid "'number grabbing' methods in favor of methods that generate problem models." Let's take a look at a guided math lesson in which the teacher encourages the students to solve problems with models.

Mr. Lee: Today we are going to work on problems where there is a change in the middle of the story. We are going to be looking for what happened. We are going to continue looking at how different models can help us solve the problem. Remember that models help us to think about a problem rather than just jumping to the solution. Here is our first problem. Marco had $155. He went to the store and bought an MP3 player. Now he has $27 left. How much money did Marco spend on his MP3 player? How could we show our thinking with a bar diagram?

Carol: It might look like this:

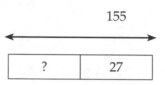

Mr. Lee: Who can explain Carol's diagram?

Tom: The 155 is at the top because we know the whole. We don't know the change so that is in the middle. The question mark means we don't know what happened. The 27 is what we know we have left.

Mr. Lee: Excellent explanation. It is always important to know what you are looking for—you have a much better chance of finding it then. Okay, so now that we have the setup, how can we solve it?

Sheila: Well, you can subtract?

Mr. Lee: Are you sure about that?

Sheila: Kinda . . . I think you can subtract because it is 27 plus something makes 155.

Mr. Lee: Okay, try it and see if it is correct.

Sheila: Yes, it works. It is 128 and that is right.

Mr. Lee: Okay, does someone have another way of modeling that problem?

David: Yes, I am going to use the open number line.

Mr. Lee: Okay, do it. But be sure to talk us through your thinking.

David: Okay. I am going to draw a line.

And then I am going to write my numbers and make jumps.

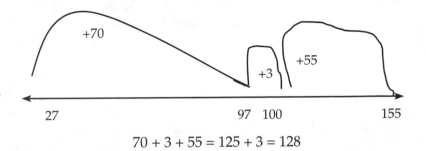

$$70 + 3 + 55 = 125 + 3 = 128$$

Mr. Lee: Does everybody agree with him?

Kyle: I would use the open number line but make different jumps.

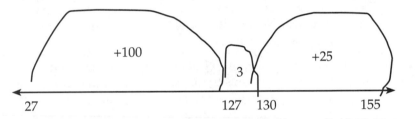

I would hop 100 and then 3 and then 25. You get the same answer but
I think it is easier to add that way.

Mr. Lee: Okay, what do you guys think?

Carla: I would add it like Marcos did because it is an easier jump.
Jumping by 100s makes it easy.

Mr. Lee: Okay, does anyone else have a different model they would
use?

Marcos: I would just count up to get close to 155. Like I would go
27 + 130 = 157 and that would be 2 over so I would then take away
2 to get back to 155. That would make 128.

Mr. Lee: Okay, that's another strategy. So we can see that we have lots
of different ways to show our thinking about a problem. In your
centers you all will be practicing how to show your thinking about
a problem. You will get a story problem and then choose a model
to solve it. Any questions? Okay, you guys can go back to your
seats.

The new Common Core State Standards for math emphasize solving
problems across the domains. Mathematical Practice 1 states that students
need to find "pathways rather than just jumping to a solution." Mathematical Practice 4 focuses on students using a variety of mathematical models
to explain their thinking. Figure 7.4 (page 92) shows just some of the content domains and grade levels that require strategic competence.

Figure 7.4 Strategic Competence in the Common Core State Standards

Content Domains: Operations & Algebraic Thinking; Number & Operations—Fractions

Kindergarten	K.OA.A.2: Solve addition and subtraction word problems, and add and subtract within 10, e.g., by using objects or drawings to represent the problem
Grade 1	1.OA.A.1: Use addition and subtraction within 20 to solve word problems involving situations of adding to, taking from, putting together, taking apart, and comparing, with unknowns in all positions, e.g., by using objects, drawings, and equations
Grade 2	2.OA.A.1: Use addition and subtraction within 100 to solve one- and two-step word problems involving situations of adding to, taking from, putting together, taking apart, and comparing, with unknowns in all positions, e.g., by using drawings and equations
Grade 3	3.OA.A.3: Use multiplication and division within 100 to solve word problems in situations involving equal groups, arrays, and measurement quantities, e.g., by using drawings and equations with a symbol for the unknown number to represent the problem
Grade 4	4.OA.A.2: Multiply or divide to solve word problems involving multiplicative comparison, e.g., by using drawings and equations with a symbol for the unknown number to represent the problem, distinguishing multiplicative comparison from additive comparison
Grade 5	5.NF.A.2: Solve word problems involving addition and subtraction of fractions referring to the same whole, including cases of unlike denominators, e.g., by using visual fraction models or equations to represent the problem

© 2010 Common Core State Standards Initiative

Adaptive Reasoning

Adaptive reasoning is one of the key components of mathematical proficiency. Students with adaptive reasoning can think logically about math and they can explain and justify what they are doing. The key to getting students to engage in mathematical discussions is to create a talk-friendly environment. It is important that students feel that what they have to say will be considered worthy and important. They need to know that they will not be mocked, ridiculed, or belittled.

One of the main purposes of meeting with students in small guided math groups is to get them talking. You want students to be able to explain their thinking out loud to a group of people who are intently listening to their words, making connections with their thoughts, and questioning them about what they are saying.

The public protocols that we refer to during whole-group discussions are just as relevant during small-group discussions. Students are encouraged to refer to these and use them. The National Research Council (2001, p. 130) notes that one important "manifestation of adaptive reasoning is the ability to justify one's work." But it clarifies that there is a difference between justifying and proving, noting that proofs are more complete, whereas justifications are less formal. Students would be expected to write down their proofs and explain them through a series of logical arguments, whereas discussing their reasoning would be sufficient for justifications. Let's take a look at a small guided math group working on adaptive reasoning.

Mrs. Feinstein: Today we are going to be working on proving it! I want you to get really good at being able to prove that what you say is true in math. Why do you think that is important?

Timothy: Because you have to check. Sometimes people say stuff that is wrong and you have to be able to show them. You have to be able to prove it.

Mrs. Feinstein: Yep. We have to prove our own thinking and be able to talk about other people's work with pictures, drawings, numbers, and words. Let's practice a problem. Say I want to prove that $5 \times 3 = 15$. Who can tell me what I might do?

Charlie You could use the number grid. You could skip count on it like we did the other day.

Mrs. Feinstein: I sure could, Charlie. Why don't you show us how?

Charlie: [picks up a number grid and whiteboard marker from the toolbox on the table; skip counts by fives, circling the numbers as he goes along] There, I did it. I used the number grid to prove it!

Mrs. Feinstein: Yep, you sure did. Does everybody agree that his way is one way to prove it? Who can talk about Charlie's way?

Marta: Yeah, it works. I agree. It's true, he landed on 15 and that's the answer.

Timothy: I agree and I have another way too. I could use the number line and do the same thing [picks up a number line and a whiteboard marker from the toolbox and demonstrates the problem]. There, I did it. I proved the answer is 15.

Mrs. Feinstein: Yep, you sure did. Who can talk about how these two boys' methods of proving it were the same and different?

Kelly: They both skip counted. They used the number line and the number grid. They didn't draw it out.

Marta: I could draw an array. It would have 5 rows and 3 columns.

Mrs. Feinstein: Can you draw it for us?

Marta: Yep. Here it is [shows her work].

Mrs. Feinstein: Very good work, everyone. Now I am going to give each one of you a flash card with a multiplication problem. Your job is to prove it in more than one way on your paper. You can collect your evidence behind your paper—for example, if you use the number grid, that would go just in back of your work as the evidence. I am going to give you a few minutes to start work on this and then we will come back together and talk about what you did. Everybody understand?

Mrs. Feinstein lets the children work for a few minutes. She takes notes on each of the ways that the children are working. She wants to think about how she can get Charlie to use other ways to prove his thinking, since he is somewhat overreliant on the number grid. After about five minutes, she brings them back together to discuss what they did. All the students share their problem and at least one way they proved it. Mrs. Feinstein asks them to compare all the ways and talk about what are some fast ways and what are some slow ways. Then, she debriefs the main points of the lesson with them.

Mrs. Feinstein: Okay, so today we talked about being able to prove your thinking. What would you say are some of the key points?

Timothy: That you can prove your thinking in lots of ways!

Marta: You can use the number grid, the number line, arrays, pictures . . .

Carlos: Circles and stars too!

Mrs. Feinstein: Is it okay just to show the way?

Charly: No, you have to explain what you did!

Mrs. Feinstein: All right, you will be working on this in your centers and for homework. I'll see you all later this week. We will continue our discussion about proving it! You can go back to your seats.

The new Common Core State Standards for math stress the importance of student reasoning throughout the content domains and the practices. There are several places across the domains and practices where students are asked to ask themselves, "Does this make sense?" Figure 7.5 is a chart that shows just some of the content domains and grade levels that require reasoning.

Mathematical Disposition

Beliefs are big. Students' beliefs about math and themselves as mathematicians "exert a powerful influence" on what students think they can do, on what they are capable of doing, on how much they will try, on how much they will stay engaged with the math, and ultimately on their mathematical

Figure 7.5 Reasoning in the Common Core State Standards

Content Domain: Number & Operations—Fractions

Grade 3	3.NF.A.3: Explain equivalence of fractions in special cases, and compare fractions by reasoning about their size
Grade 4	4.NF.B.3b: Justify decompositions, e.g., by using a visual fraction model. Examples: $\frac{3}{8} = \frac{1}{8} + \frac{1}{8} + \frac{1}{8}$; $\frac{3}{8} = \frac{1}{8} + \frac{2}{8}$; $2\frac{1}{8} = 1 + 1 + \frac{1}{8} = \frac{8}{8} + \frac{8}{8} + \frac{1}{8}$
Grade 5	5.NF.A.2: Use benchmark fractions and number sense of fractions to estimate mentally and assess the reasonableness of answers. For example, recognize an incorrect result $\frac{2}{5} + \frac{1}{2} = \frac{3}{7}$ by observing that $\frac{3}{7} < \frac{1}{2}$

disposition (NCTM, 1989, p. 233). Because we know that there is a definite relationship between what students believe and teaching and learning, we have to think about how we as teachers take this into account when teaching math. By third grade, students have really ingrained beliefs about themselves as learners in all curriculum areas because they have had ample experiences. So they believe either that they are really good at something or that they "suck"! Given these mathematical autobiographies, how do we shape, or in many cases unshape and reshape, their mathematical dispositions? How do we help shift students' negative belief systems about math and themselves as learners?

Much has been written about mathematical dispositions or ways of thinking and being (NCTM, 1989, 2000; De Corte, Verschaffel, & Op 't Eynde, 2000; McIntosh, 2009; Polya, 1957). The research tells us that mathematical disposition is much more than an attitude. It is about ways of thinking, doing, being, and seeing math. It includes confidence, flexibility, perseverance, interest, inventiveness, appreciation, reflection, and monitoring (Merz, 2009).

In small guided math groups, teachers need to do several things to cultivate these components of mathematical dispositions. We can boost students' confidence by giving scaffolded "just-right" problems that they can solve successfully. They may have to stretch, but they can do the problems. Success breeds success and confidence. We can foster flexibility by talking about more than one way to do something within a culture of sharing that goes beyond the answer to discuss how students got the answer or didn't get it.

Small-group instruction also encourages perseverance by allowing students the time to "wrestle with the problem." I tell them that sometimes they have to struggle before they get there and that's okay. I call these types of problems "wiggly" because they just seem to wiggle out of the students' reach for a bit. We talk about what it means to stick with a problem . . . to persevere.

We tap into children's natural interest by making connections to their real lives. We talk about the math involved in Pokeman and Dragonball Z. We look at the math used in the school and at home. We also encourage inventiveness and an appreciation of math. We publicly celebrate inventive thinking. We encourage risk taking and leaps of faith: students don't know what will happen but they try it anyway. This feels safer for some students in a small guided math group, where they are much more willing to take risks.

Students should always be given the opportunity to reflect about the math they are learning. We should consistently use entrance and/or exit slips so they can think about their learning. We should use individual pupil responses like thumbs up, thumbs down, or thumbs sideways to check in with them. We can use green, yellow, and red slips so they can give us immediate feedback about speeding up the lesson, slowing down the lesson, or stopping to explain further. These methods are very much connected with getting students to monitor their learning. In groups there should be time for all students to talk about what they are working on personally. Students should be working toward individual mathematical goals.

Summary

Guided math groups are the perfect space to build mathematical proficiency. Teachers can take their time to build conceptual understanding, check for procedural fluency, and give students the opportunity to talk and show their thinking. Students get to try a variety of strategies and discuss what is efficient and what is not. Students can reason out loud, listen to others, and then synthesize all that information to see if it really makes sense to them. They also get to engage as mathematicians, building their own confidence and competence, taking risks, sharing ideas, and showing their work in a setting that thrives on opportunity.

Reflection Questions

1. How much time do you spend on building conceptual understanding of the topics you teach?
2. How much time do you build in for students to prove their thinking in more than one way? How might you improve on this?
3. Do you have a culture of reasoning in your classroom? How would you describe it?
4. Think about the problem-solving culture in your classroom. Do students model their thinking with numbers, words, and pictures?
5. What is the mathematical disposition of your students? What might you do to build it?

8

What Are the Other Kids Doing?

Guided math is a great structure IF you set it up correctly. The key is that everybody knows what to do. The real challenge is to make sure everyone is meaningfully engaged so that the teacher can teach the guided math group. In a balanced mathematics classroom, independent practice is a critical element.

Math Centers

Math centers allow students to concretize their knowledge and intensively practice their math skills. In order for this to happen, teachers have to plan for differentiated, standards-based, engaging independent practice. First of all, remember that, despite the name, math centers are an activity, not a particular place in the classroom. Often math centers take place at a student's own desk. Students just pick up the centers in a bucket or envelope, gather together in a space, and get to work.

There are several factors that make math centers run smoothly. First, you should hang math anchor charts prominently in the room (see Figure 8.1, page 100). Math anchor charts remind students of what they should be doing during student activity time. Often these posters are written in "I can" language.

Second, center storage should be easy, organized, and durable. Baskets, envelopes, pails, and bins are all useful containers, depending on the center (see Figure 8.2, page 101). These containers should include everything needed for that center—cards, dice, templates, spinners, game boards, and other supplies—so students can begin their work immediately. The containers should be stored someplace that is manageable so they are easy to get out and easy to put back.

Third, math centers must be planned so that students are able to do the work independently without the teacher's constant presence. They can practice alone, with a partner, or with a group. The work should be in the students' zone of proximal development (Vygotsky, 1978). Often, teachers

Figure 8.1 Math Workstation Anchor Charts

give all the students the same work because planning for different centers can seem overwhelming. When all students are given the same work, some can do it and others can't. When students can't do the work, they get off task and disrupt the learning environment for everyone. The goal is for all students to be doing work that improves their skills and allows them to practice and self-check their work.

Centers usually last between 10 and 15 minutes. I have the students play games in rounds of five turns. In this way, everyone stays engaged. Otherwise, if Carlos had 100 points and Trevor had 2 points halfway through a game, Trevor would have no incentive to keep playing because he would know that he was probably going to lose. But, if the students are playing five rounds, Carlos might win this round but Trevor might win the next. I find that rounds keep students engaged.

Grouping

There are many different ways that students can work in math centers. I suggest you have your students work in a variety of groupings throughout the week, including individual work, partner work, and group work. Sometimes these groups can be homogeneous and other times they can be heterogeneous, depending on what the students are doing. For example, if they are working on a specific skill, strategy, or concept, they probably

Figure 8.2 Storage Ideas

Decorated buckets can be convenient center holders.	Labeled bins can be easy center storage items. These bins contain different activities and the manipulatives required for each.	Labeled milk crates also provide useful math center storage. You can use them to store either plastic bags or envelopes with materials for the different math centers.	Magazine holders also make great center holders. You might put the centers in envelopes, bags, or folders inside this system.
Plastic shoe containers with lids also work well. To save space, make sure to get ones that can be stacked.	Hanging center containers can be used too.	There are also really cool expandable files that open up and create great accessible storage space.	Small plastic bins can work as well.

will be in a homogeneous group. But if they are working on a class Big Book, a class mural, or some other class project, they probably will be in a heterogeneous group because this type of work is more general. If, for example, you designate Fridays as class project days, students would work in heterogeneous groups. Also, you might want to pick one day a week that is free-choice day when students can work in heterogeneous groups.

It is important to note, however, that even if they are in heterogeneous groups, students are still working with "just-right" center activities. For example, if John chooses to work out of the Geometry Bin, he still chooses the activities for the Trapezoids group because that is the level he is working on at the time. So on free-choice day John would work with other students who wanted to work out of the Geometry Bin, but they are all working on different activities from their designated bags.

Individual Work

Students can work individually on certain tasks. For example, they can practice their basic arithmetic facts by playing with dice, dominos, or a deck of cards. They should have some sort of sheet to record the work they are doing. Often, although students are working individually, they are sitting in a group. This is parallel work, where they are working on the same task but not together.

Partner Work

There are different types of partner work. Students can work playing either collaborative games or competitive games. There should be a mix of both kinds.

Collaborative Games

Students will often work with partners during center time. It is important to spend time at the beginning of the year talking about what it means to be a good partner. Students might play a collaborative game with a partner, both working toward a particular goal (see Figure 8.3). For example, putting together puzzles can be done as partner work. Working together to match fraction numbers with pictures cards is another example of a collaborative partner game.

Competitive Games

Other times, students will play a competitive game with their partner. For example, in Addition War, partners play against each other to see who will get the most pairs of cards. In Highest Number, partners pull cards and compare them. Whoever has the highest number gets to keep the cards.

Team Games

Sometimes students will play with a partner as a team against another team. For example, in Add to 100, they play together as a team to get to 100 first. Students can play games in teams on the computer as well.

Group Work

Group work can be either collaborative or competitive. It is good to have students play both of these types of games. Remember that learning is socialized, and when students work together they can gain and reinforce a great deal of content and skill knowledge. Groups can play games, solve word problems, and practice facts, among other things.

Collaborative Work

Sometimes the students work in groups at their centers. An example of a group activity is solving a word problem collaboratively. Each person has a role to play in solving the word problem. The students pick a word problem from a list, out of a hat, or from an activity sheet. They then either

Figure 8.3 Power Towers for Fluency Practice

Tower group games are fun! Students pick cups with math facts (for example, "3 × 3") and try to build the tallest tower that they can by getting the facts correct!

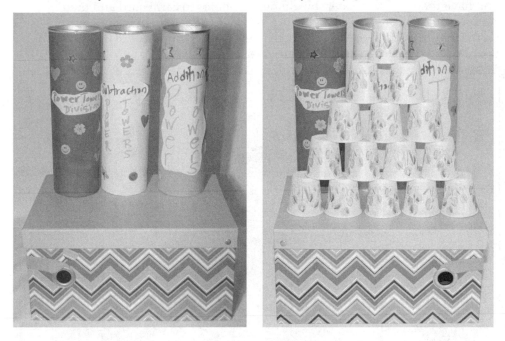

choose or are assigned roles. One person is the reader. One person is the illustrator. One person is the number cruncher. One person is the checker. They then solve the problem. The reader reads the problem and translates it for the others. The illustrator draws a model to show their thinking about the problem. The number cruncher writes an equation to show the numbers in the problem. The checker solves the problem in a different way in order to check the original solution.

Competitive Games
Students can also play games together in groups where they are trying to win. Board games, card games, and domino games are examples of competitive games. Students like these games and they stay engaged. I often use games like this to reinforce basic operations and knowledge of money or time.

Types of Centers

There are many different types of centers that you might consider using in your class. Here are seven must-have centers.

Figure 8.4 Showcasing Student Work

What do you do to showcase your students' great work? Here is a great idea—student math magnets! At the beginning of the year, take pictures of each student and have them make magnets by gluing the photos to cardboard and then putting magnets on the back of them. You can also have them include captions on the magnets (below). Allow students to post their work to a math bulletin board using their magnets. Talk about student ownership!

This is my work I put on the bulletin board. I am very proud of it.

#1: Basic Fact Center

You want to be sure to have a center where students can practice their basic math facts. In this center, they can quiz each other on flash cards or sort the flash cards by specific strategies. For example, if they picked 8 + 7, they might sort that into a Lucky 8 pile because they know they can make any 8 a 10 and add fast. They could also sort that fact into a "doubles plus or minus 1" pile.

#2: Hot Topics Review Center

In this center students review all the skills that they have worked on during the year so far and even skills from the previous year. Students practice money, time, rounding, graphing, and concepts skills in this center. Sometimes I tell the students what they have to work on in this center, but often I let them choose their own topics. I tell them to think about what they need to practice and get better at doing.

Figure 8.5 Dice

It is unreasonable to expect to change and differentiate centers every week, so many of your centers should be standards-based activities that students can play several times. If you have a good center, then your students can revisit it many times and practice at different levels. So you can have a basic center that is differentiated by levels.

For example, I use dice in many centers. Students can do addition, subtraction, multiplication, division, place value, time, and measurement activities with dice.

#3: Geometry Center

Geometry is a very big part of the primary curriculum. The research states that most students do not learn much geometry beyond what they already come to school knowing, and that teachers should complexify their students' geometric understandings by discussing and designing multiple experiences with different types of polygons (besides regular ones). Students often will say that anything that isn't green and equilateral isn't a triangle or that any hexagon that doesn't look like the one in the pattern blocks box isn't a hexagon. So you need to have plenty of center activities that deepen their understanding of the attributes of two-dimensional shapes. I encourage teachers to put up a geometry center with Play-Doh, paint, blocks, and scaffolded activities where students can build and explore the attributes of shapes at a more complex level as the year progresses.

#4: Word Problem Center

According to the research, there are four basic types of addition and subtraction problems with three subtypes each and nine types of multiplication and division problems with one subtype each. These are a lot of problem types to explore throughout the year (see Figure 8.6, page 106). In a problem-solving center, students can explore problems at the concrete, pictorial, and abstract level. They can take their time, think about the problems, and act them out with manipulatives, felt, and magnets. They can also write about their problem-solving process and model their thinking. I highly encourage teachers to have a problem-solving center with problems that take more than two minutes to solve.

#5: Math Poem Center

This is a fun interdisciplinary center. I believe in using math poems, math songs, and math picture books. In this center, students work on a project

Figure 8.6 Student Work

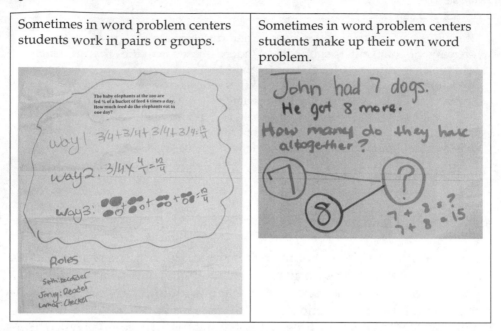

Sometimes in word problem centers students work in pairs or groups.	Sometimes in word problem centers students make up their own word problem.

associated with one of these things that we are doing in class. For instance, they might work on individual versions of a poem or a story. They could also be working on a class math Big Book of a story or poem. They might be working on number writing. Poems help math to come alive.

#6: Math Journal Center

A math journal center can have students doing very powerful work. In the math journal, the students can explore concepts, work on projects, and really do some high-quality thinking. I encourage teachers to think of math journals as thinking notebooks that help students grapple with mathematical issues. Interactive math journals are an excellent tool for students to showcase their thinking. In these math journals, students make flipbooks, and accordion foldouts and pop-up illustrations of vocabulary to illustrate the math topics they are studying.

#7: Math Vocabulary Center

Math is a language and students need to know the words to be able to speak it. When teachers tell students to use their math words, they need to know which words to use. A math vocabulary center offers many ways to practice the words from prior units of study as well as engage with the words from the current unit of study. The students can play bingo, tic-tac-toe, match, and concentration as well as do word finds and crossword puzzles. There are also web 2.0 sites where they can make digital math vocabulary flash cards and play math vocabulary games.

Math Center Logistics

There are many different types of things that you can do to ensure that your math centers run smoothly. For example, make sure that you have standards-based task cards, scaffolded worksheets, leveled centers, and student reflection sheets.

Using Standards-Based Task Cards

All the math centers should be directly connected to a standard. On the task card, I write down the math that students will be practicing, the procedure, and the rules. Often, I put pictures on the task cards so students have a pictorial reminder of what happens in that center (see Figure 8.7). On the back I write the standard.

Figure 8.7 Task Cards

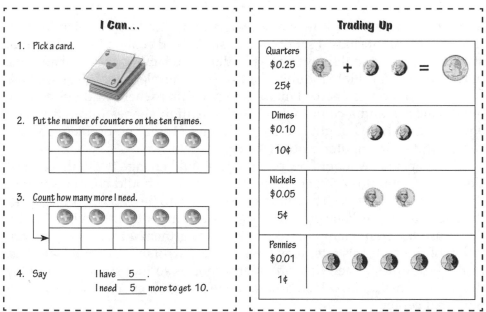

Examples of Task Cards

I Can...

1. Pick a card.

2. Put the number of counters on the ten frames.

3. Count how many more I need.

4. Say   I have ___5___ .
                I need ___5___ more to get 10.

Trading Up

Quarters
$0.25
25¢

Dimes
$0.10
10¢

Nickels
$0.05
5¢

Pennies
$0.01
1¢

Figure 8.8 Scaffolded Task Cards

Race to 100

Yeah, you won!	Remember to regroup when all ten are covered!	Remember to regroup when all ten are covered!
	10 tens = 1 hundred	10 ones = 1 ten

Using Scaffolded Activity Sheets

Scaffolded organizers are really important. They help students to know what to do. They give written and picture clues so that students can engage in the game more efficiently. I especially like them for trading games with base-ten blocks and money because students get clues about when to make the trades (see Figure 8.8).

Using Leveled Centers

Many teachers wonder how many centers they should use. I plan for centers by the unit of study. I set up five or six leveled centers for each unit of study. I choose from the seven basic centers listed above and then add one or two centers specific to the unit of study. For example, if a third-grade class is doing a unit on geometry, I might set up a center where students explore quadrilaterals and a center where they partition shapes into pairs with equal areas. Then, I might use the hot topics center, the problem-solving center, and the computer center. (See Figure 8.9.)

Teachers also wonder how often they should change the math centers. Centers are about practicing for proficiency. You should change some of the centers every week. This chore doesn't have to be overwhelming. Take the above example. You could change the fraction center by having the students use different manipulatives or by giving them a pictorial representation of the materials after they have worked with the concrete materials. In the hot topics center, there are many choices so that students can play different games and work on different review topics every time they work with that center.

Figure 8.9 Math Center Planning Sheet

Math Centers

Big Ideas: Shapes can be composed and decomposed into smaller and larger shapes
Standards: Geometry Domain 3G CCSS

	Center 1: Quadrilaterals	Center 2: Dividing Shapes into Equal Parts	Center 3: Hot Topics	Center 4: Problem-Solving Center	Center 5: Computer Center Games
Novice	Tiered graphic organizer exploring attributes of quadrilaterals	Exploring halves and quarters with fraction circles	Free choice: time, money, or fact match	Using fraction circles to solve stories	Choice 1: Make a shape with virtual manipulatives
Apprentice		Exploring halves, quarters, and eighths with fraction squares		Using fraction squares to solve stories	Choice 2: Shape Game
Practitioner		Exploring halves, quarters, eighths, fifths, and tenths with fraction bars		Using fraction bars to solve stories	
Expert		Exploring all the fractions on the fraction bars			

Figure 8.10 Math Workshop Schedule

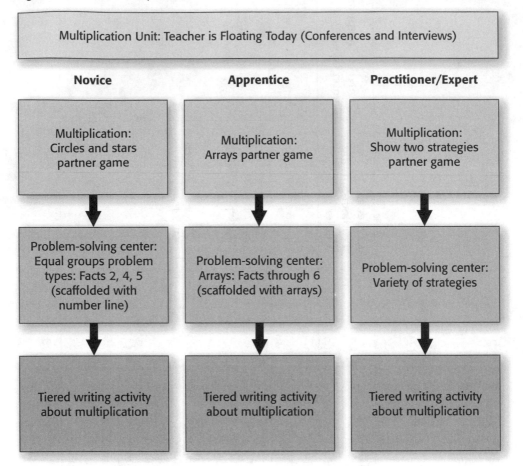

Multiplication Unit: Teacher is Floating Today (Conferences and Interviews)		
Novice	**Apprentice**	**Practitioner/Expert**
Multiplication: Circles and stars partner game	Multiplication: Arrays partner game	Multiplication: Show two strategies partner game
Problem-solving center: Equal groups problem types: Facts 2, 4, 5 (scaffolded with number line)	Problem-solving center: Arrays: Facts through 6 (scaffolded with arrays)	Problem-solving center: Variety of strategies
Tiered writing activity about multiplication	Tiered writing activity about multiplication	Tiered writing activity about multiplication

Holding Students Accountable

Students should be held accountable for the work they do during center time. All students should have a folder where they keep the artifacts of the games they play and the work they do. At the end of math period, the students should share some of their work, using the written record as examples during their conversation. Also, sometime during the week the teacher should look through the folders to see what each student is doing. The teacher can leave notes on the sheets for the students. Figure 8.10 shows a sample schedule for a day when the teacher is not doing a guided math group and all the students are working in centers.

Figure 8.11 shows examples of all the centers that the students would be going to during the week while a guided math lesson is happening. One thing to notice about the centers is they are differentiated by task and knowledge levels. So everyone is working with basically the same

Figure 8.11 Unit Center Planning Sheet

Place Value Centers

Novices They will be working with two-digit numbers	Base-ten blocks: Build a number (Roll and Build)	Magnetic base-ten blocks (Pull a Card and Make a Number)	Stamp base-ten blocks: Use template	Find different ways: Match word, number	Spin 10 More or Less Game
Apprentices They will be working with two digit numbers	Base-ten blocks: Build a number (Roll and Build)	Magnetic base-ten blocks (Pull a Card and Make a Number)	Stamp base-ten blocks: Use template	Find different ways: Match word, number	Spin 10 More or Less Game
Practitioners They will be working with one- to three-digit numbers	Base-ten blocks: Build a number (Roll and Build)	Magnetic base-ten blocks (Pull a Card and Make a Number)	Stamp base-ten blocks: Use template	Find different ways: Match word, number, expanded form	Spin 10 or 100 More or Less Game
Experts They will be working with one- to three-digit numbers and possibly four-digit numbers	Base-ten blocks: Build a number (Roll and Build)	Magnetic base-ten blocks (Pull a Card and Make a Number)	Stamp base-ten blocks: Use template	Find different ways: Match word, number, expanded form	Spin 10 or 100 More or Less Game

Figure 8.12 Math Station Self Checks

materials, but the activities that they are practicing vary according to knowledge and skill levels.

Giving Feedback on Math Center Work

It is important to reinforce good behavior during math workshop as well as have students reflect on their own behavior. Figure 8.12 suggests a few helpful ideas.

Reflecting on Math Center Work

Often teachers ask students to reflect on their math center work. Students can write this reflection in their math journals or on a reflection sheet (see Figure 8.13). Students can reflect verbally, but I would also have them do it in written form at least once or twice during the week.

Figure 8.13 Sample Reflection Sheets

Sample Reflection Sheets

Today in math center I did . . .	Today in math center I played with . . . We played . . . We were practicing . . .	Today in math center my group . . . This is what I learned:

Summary

Center work is about students engaging in purposeful practice, sometimes individually, but often in pairs and groups. Centers work well when explicit protocols have been established and students are accountable for the work they are doing. It shouldn't take an inordinate amount of time to create centers. You should create centers around Big Ideas and then differentiate the tasks that students work on around that Big Idea.

Reflection Questions

1. How often do you currently give students the opportunity to practice on their own, in pairs, and in groups?
2. How do you presently hold your students accountable for the work they are doing?
3. What do you think are the hot topics at your grade level that you want your students to practice throughout the year?

9

The First 20 Days of Math Workshop: Setting the Stage for Effective Guided Math Groups

Rolling out the first 20 days of math workshop in your own classroom will take time, persistence, and consistency. Here is a 20-day plan to get you started. Taking the time to establish the routines is well worth the energy and the effort. You want students to know what math workshop looks like, how to act in the workshop, and how to work independently throughout the workshop. If you spend the time in the beginning of the year to lay a strong foundation, then students can get on with learning together in productive ways.

Students will need to learn what to do during the mini-lesson, how to work with whiteboards for individual responses, how to take notes in the whole-group setting, and how to participate with each other. They will also need to learn how to work together during workstations. These lessons will focus on working independently, with partners, and in groups. Students will learn how to get workstations out, play with them, and then put them away. They will need to learn when they can talk to the teacher and when they cannot interrupt her.

During the first 20 days of math workshop, you will emphasize mathematical practices that are the "habits of mind" and "ways of being" that students will need in order to become proficient mathematicians. There are eight practices (CCSS, 2012) to lay the groundwork for during this period.

1. Make sense of problems and persevere in solving them.
2. Reason abstractly and quantitatively.
3. Construct viable arguments and critique the reasoning of others.
4. Model with mathematics.
5. Use appropriate tools strategically.
6. Attend to precision.
7. Look for and make use of structure.
8. Look for and express regularity in repeated reasoning.

You will teach your students to

1. become public mathematicians and to listen, read, write, and speak together in order to learn math
2. work together around a specific set of routines and procedures during math workshop

The First 20 Days of Guided Math chart (Figure 9.9, page 128) outlines a very specific framework for laying out the work at the beginning of the year. It includes essential questions, enduring understandings, skills, assessments, and sample math anchor charts. Teachers should individualize these ideas to fit their individual teaching styles.

Every class, every year is different. Some years you will spend more time on one section than in other years. You will move the sections around to fit your own style and rhythm. Do what works best for your class. Make it work! Make it comfortable for yourself! As Fountas and Pinnell (2001) point out, "Lessons build on each other; points are repeated; charts are posted in the room and referred to again and again." Take your time. Emphasize the key routines over and over again.

The First Week

During the first week you will set the context for the work you will do all year. You will orient the students to math workshop. You will have various discussions about what good mathematicians do. You will emphasize the idea that mathematicians talk and listen to each other, they share their thinking and ask questions, and they show their thinking as well.

Day 1: What Is Math Workshop?

The goal of this session is to introduce the students to math workshop. You will explain the general structure and discuss the overall routines and procedures, such as calendar; number talks; the mini-lesson; student activity time, when workstations and guided math groups take place, as well as student interviews and conferences; and finally the debrief. The students should engage in a prolonged discussion of the workshop and the way they are going to think about and do math throughout the year. The teacher should create some sort of math anchor chart that highlights the discussion (see Figure 9.1).

Day 2: How Do Good Mathematicians Communicate with Each Other?

The goal of this session is to talk about talk. You want to begin the discussion about the ways public mathematicians engage with each other. Students need to learn that good mathematicians talk and listen to each

Figure 9.1 Math Workshop Anchor Chart

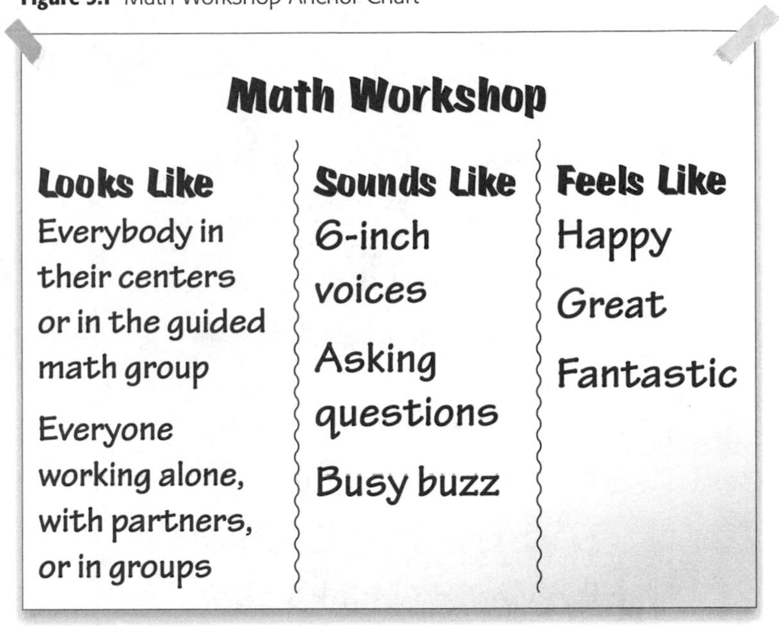

Math Workshop

Looks Like

Everybody in their centers or in the guided math group

Everyone working alone, with partners, or in groups

Sounds Like

6-inch voices

Asking questions

Busy buzz

Feels Like

Happy

Great

Fantastic

other. Students learn to make eye contact and be attentive and to respond with a thinking mind and a respectful heart. They learn about "think time" (see Figure 9.2, page 120). They learn to allow each other the time and space to speak, to stop and think about what has been said, and then to digest that and think some more before they respond. The focus of this session is to teach students to respect each other. It is also to get students to begin to talk about word problems. So you introduce a Problem of the Day and practice using think time to discuss it.

Day 3: How Do Good Mathematicians Talk About Their Ideas?

The third day is a continuation of the conversation about being a good mathematician. Students discuss the idea that math is a language and that one of the things that they will work on during math workshop is "speaking math." A math anchor chart about how to talk with each other and respond to questions can be a part of this discussion (see Figure 9.3, page 121). The teacher should introduce the *word wall* that will help students remember the words they are learning. They also may play some vocabulary games, as an example of the types of games that they will play all year to learn new math words.

Students learn to use different prompts to share their thinking about math. You can chart some of these ideas and have the class practice using them. Students learn to speak about their mathematical thinking by actually speaking about math! Using more math word problems as the center of the discussion, students practice talking with each other.

Figure 9.2 Think Time Anchor Chart

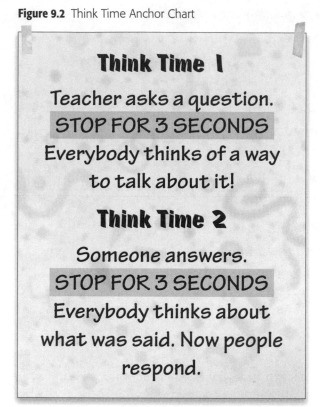

Day 4: How Do Good Mathematicians Show Their Work?

The fourth day is about students learning that good mathematicians show their work (see Figure 9.4). You want to spend some time talking with students about asking questions. Students need to get comfortable with asking questions of themselves and others. The discussion should focus on what "showing work" looks like. Students should understand that they can show their work with objects, drawings, and pictures, and also through acting it out. In order to focus on this point, students do more work with the Problem of the Day.

Day 5: How Do Good Mathematicians Write?

The fifth day is about writing in math class. During this session, students focus on different ways to write in math class. You introduce the class journal for the first time during the debrief. Students talk about how, during this time, they will write about the math that they did. You also introduce math journals and have the students make them. The journals have different sections, such as vocabulary, do-now, and word problems. The number of sections depends on the grade level of your class.

Figure 9.3 How to Talk About Math

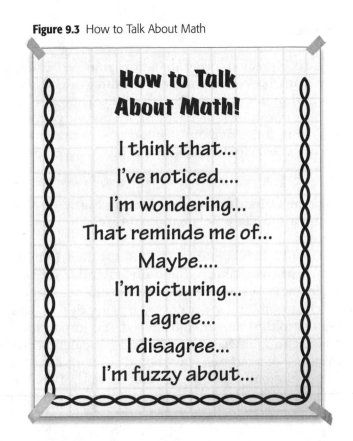

How to Talk
About Math!

I think that...
I've noticed....
I'm wondering...
That reminds me of...
Maybe....
I'm picturing...
I agree...
I disagree...
I'm fuzzy about...

Figure 9.4 Showing Your Work Anchor Chart

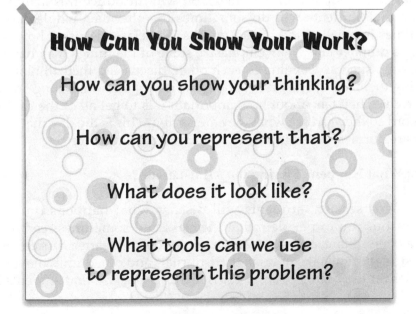

How Can You Show Your Work?

How can you show your thinking?

How can you represent that?

What does it look like?

What tools can we use
to represent this problem?

The Second Week

The second week is about exploring the initial routines, rules, and procedures. Students learn how to use their individual calendars. They learn how to engage in number talks with each other. They also learn how to actively participate in mini-lessons. During this week you also introduce math centers. During these five days, students can practice the routines and become secure in exactly what to do during the work period/student activity time.

Day 6: What Are the Calendar Routines During Math Workshop and How Do They Relate to Real Life?

This session is about establishing one of the routines that students will practice during math workshop—the daily calendar routine. Students will discuss different types of calendars and examine a regular calendar as well as the "classroom" calendar posted in the calendar area. Here the individual calendar folders are also introduced. It is important for students to make the connection between real life and the calendar routines that they will do in class. For example, why should students chart the weather? In real life, do people really follow the weather and, if so, when, where, and why? Contextualizing our daily math routines is essential to students being able to make sense of math in their world.

Day 7: How Do We Participate in Number Talks?

This session is about number talks. You will introduce this activity as a routine that students will do sometimes together as a whole class and sometimes in small guided math groups. The class discusses how to talk during a number talk. They emphasize some of the things they have been discussing, such as listening to each other, discussing their thinking, and showing their work. They talk about how it is okay to be wrong and okay to be right. They talk about how important it is to get all of their thinking on record so they can see what they are saying. This is the day that the students are normed into this routine, through actual practice.

Day 8: What Happens During the Mini-Lesson?

During this session, students will discuss what happens during the mini-lesson. You can explain that the class will sometimes read a book; learn a poem, chant, or song; watch a mini-video; or learn a concept. Sometimes students will take notes in their journals and other times they will do activities on their whiteboards. You should emphasize that students have

Figure 9.5 Playing Games Anchor Chart

Important Things When Playing Games

1. Take turns

2. Play fairly

3. Record what happens

4. Put everything BACK in the bag

5. Be happy

a really important role during the mini-lesson—to listen, talk with each other, and participate.

Day 9: How Do We Work at Math Centers?

This session focuses on introducing math centers to the students. You will spend a great deal of time rolling out math centers over the next few days. Students need to learn to take out the math centers and to work by themselves, with partners, and in groups. They need to set some rules for getting along, working well together, and resolving any problems that come up (see Figure 9.5). This takes time to do but is essential to running a great math workshop.

Day 10: How Do We Work and Play Together During Math Workshop? (Part 1)

During this session, the class continues to explore what it means to work together during student activity time. They discuss what types of

Figure 9.6 How to Start a Game

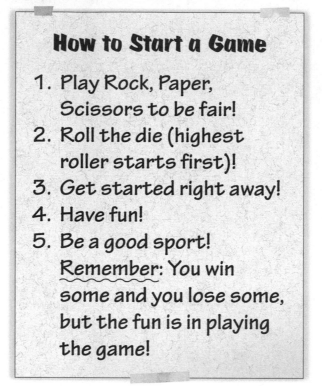

How to Start a Game

1. Play Rock, Paper, Scissors to be fair!
2. Roll the die (highest roller starts first)!
3. Get started right away!
4. Have fun!
5. Be a good sport! Remember: You win some and you lose some, but the fun is in playing the game!

manipulatives they will use when playing games and doing activities. The teacher leads a discussion about playing with partners. The class models this by breaking into two teams and playing some games. Part of this discussion is about how to start a game (see Figure 9.6). We play many different math games, but there are some general procedures for starting any type of game. Although this concept seems simple, many students struggle with it in the beginning. Students do not tend to play board games these days, so they are not used to deciding who gets to start. So it is important for students to practice it during the next few days.

The Third Week

During the third week, you will continue focusing on work in math centers and, eventually, if students are ready that week, you will start pulling guided math groups. You should work on these procedures for a few days. It is important to keep reinforcing the routines about using manipulatives, playing games, and working together (see Figure 9.7). Students should practice getting out and putting back the workstations. They should also

Figure 9.7 How to Be a Great Partner

How to be a great partner

Look
- Look at the game
- Pay attention to the game
- Watch during your partners turn
- Listen to each other

Sound
- Ask helpful questions
- Say answers
- Check answers
- Say nice things
- Use 6-inch voices

Feel
- Great!
- Fantastic!
- Supercalifragilistic-expialidocious!
- Sometimes you win, sometimes you lose!

Remember
- It's only a game!
- The fun is playing!
- We get "smarter" every time we play!

continue to practice problem solving by themselves so that when an issue comes up, they have the tools to work it out without necessarily getting the teacher involved.

Day 11: How Do We Work and Play Together During Math Workshop? (Part 2)

During this session, the students will practice playing with cards. Card games are fun and fast. They play with a variety of cards, big, little, playing cards, number cards, and flash cards. They talk about the different games that are possible with cards. They practice holding cards, shuffling cards, and dealing cards. During this session, depending on the students, students play a team game and a group game. Sometimes, the class will spend a few days on this topic, with a few days on team games and a few days on group games.

Day 12: How Do We Work and Play Together During Math Workshop? (Part 3)

During this session you introduce more manipulatives, highlighting the use of dominos for playing different games. You explain that sometimes students will use playing mats for dominos and sometimes they will not. Students then play domino games with partners and in groups. The more time that you give students to practice playing together and focusing in on the math during this week, the better they will be able to do it when the class goes into full workshop mode.

Day 13: How Do We Use Math Tools During Math Workshop?

During this session, students spend a great deal of time talking about other tools that they can use in math workshop, besides dice, dominos, and cards. They talk about unifix cubes, bears, color tiles, calculators, and other tools available in the classroom. They spend time talking about management routines concerning the tools, playing with the tools, and specifically using the tools to do math. It is important that time is spent discussing what math tools are and how they help us do math. During this session, students might also start putting together their own toolkits.

Days 14–15: What Happens During the Student Work Period of Math Workshop?

This is a key session. Guided math groups are introduced and the teacher begins to pull the first group. The students are all very aware that they are to be on their best behavior and are to do all the things they have been practicing over the last few days. There is usually a great deal of buzz and excitement on this day when they actually experience the full workshop in action. The teacher must be sure to debrief this session in detail so students know exactly what went well and what they need to work on.

The Fourth Week

Finally, during the fourth week, you will start to work on what happens during the debrief, specifically how to participate in the class journal discussion. During this time you will also introduce the Mathematician's Chair. After all the routines have been learned, be sure to spend a few days doing the workshop and talking about what is going well and what needs to improve.

Days 16–17: What Happens During Share Time at the End of Math Workshop?

During these sessions, students will discuss what happens during the debrief. It is important for them to summarize their learnings for the day and keep a public record of them. The discussion should focus on the math they did, not just the game or activity that they did. Students make anchor charts to remind them what happens during the debrief. They talk about the importance of the Mathematician's Chair and how it is an honor to share their thoughts with others. They talk about how it feels to sit in the

Mathematician's Chair and how to treat the people who sit in it. They talk about and practice sharing their work with each other.

Days 18–20: What Are the Routines, Rules, and Procedures During Math Workshop?

During these last three sessions, the class spends time doing the math workshop and talking about it extensively. This is the time to praise the good and work out the kinks and the rough spots. This is the blueprint for your yearlong journey. These last few days are meant to make sure that the foundation for math workshop is solid. The 20-day framework is just a guideline. Every class is different. Creating a vibrant, energetic, academically rigorous math workshop takes time, energy, and much effort, but it is well worth it! Stick with the process of establishing the workshop, don't get discouraged, lean into the rough spots, and know that when it is all done, you will have created a space for learning that is student centered, standards-based, and cognitively engaging and demanding. Consistency is the key. Math workshop is a great structure. Math centers are a good place to engage in purposeful practice. Guided math will change not only your teaching life but the learning lives of those you teach! Go for it!

Figure 9.8 Good Mathematicians Anchor Chart

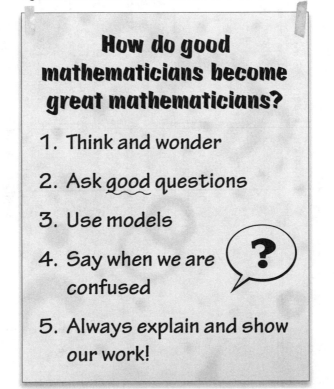

Figure 9.9 The First 20 Days of Guided Math

		Getting Started: Week 1			
Day	Focus Questions	Enduring Understandings/Content	Skills	Assessments	Activities
1	What is math workshop?	You get better at math by practicing math every day. Math workshop is a time when we work on math. Math workshop has several parts: calendar, number talks, mini-lesson, math workstations, and share time.	Be able to describe math workshop.	Class discussion	Class discussion/ Chart with flow of math workshop
2	How do good mathematicians communicate with each other?	Good mathematicians talk and listen to each other. They are respectful. They ask questions of themselves and others. They give each other "think time." **Focus on respect. Introduce the Problem of the Day.**	Be able to discuss what listening and being respectful means.	Class discussion/ drawing	Class chart
3	How do good mathematicians talk about their ideas?	Good mathematicians talk about their thinking. They use math words. They ask questions of themselves and others. **Focus on Word Wall. Continue working with the Problem of the Day.**	Talk about a problem.	Class discussion	Class chart on the language of engagement

Figure 9.9 The First 20 Days of Guided Math *(continued)*

Day	Essential Questions	Big Ideas/Content	Skills	Assessments	Activities
4	What do good mathematicians do?	Good mathematicians show their work. They ask questions of themselves and others. **Focus on showing work with objects, drawings, pictures, and acting it out. Continue working with the Problem of the Day.**	Show thinking about a problem.	Student work	Class chart
5	How do good mathematicians write about their math thinking?	Good mathematicians write about their thinking. **Focus on Writing. Continue working with the Problem of the Day.**	Write about a problem.	Student work	Student journals are introduced.
Getting Started: Week 2					
6	What are the calendar routines during math workshop and how do they relate to real life?	There are certain routines that we practice during math workshop. There are particular ways of doing things during math workshop. **Focus on calendar.**	Fill out individual calendars and graphs.	Calendar pages	Complete individual calendar

Figure 9.9 The First 20 Days of Guided Math *(continued)*

7	What are ways that we participate in number talks during Math Workshop?	There are certain routines that we practice during math workshop. There are particular ways of doing things during math workshop. **Focus on number talks.**	Participate in a discussion about numbers.	Teacher observation	Class discussion
8	What happens during the mini-lesson?	There are certain routines that we practice during math workshop. There are particular ways of doing things during math workshop. **Focus on whole-class mini-lesson.**	Actively participate in whole-class discussion.	Teacher observation	Class discussion
9	How do we work together during math work stations?	There are certain routines that we practice during math workshop. There are particular ways of doing things during math workshop. **Focus on math workstations.**	Transition to math centers. Work productively in math centers with partners.	Teacher observation/ Center work artifacts	Two games/ Chart about center work
10	How do we work and play together during math workshop?	There are certain routines that we practice during math workshop. There are particular ways of doing things during math workshop. **Focus on math workstations. Discuss using dice.**	Transition to math centers. Work productively in math centers with partners.	Teacher observation/ Center work artifacts	Two games/ Add to chart about center work

Figure 9.9 The First 20 Days of Guided Math *(continued)*

		Getting Started: Week 3			
Day	Daily Questions	Big Ideas/Content	Skills	Assessments	Activities
11	How do we work and play together during math workshop?	There are certain routines that we practice during math workshop. There are particular ways of doing things during math workshop. **Focus on math centers.** **Discuss using cards.**	Transition to centers; engage in center work; practice working with a partner.	Center artifacts	Two games
12	How do we work and play together during math workshop?	There are certain routines that we practice during math workshop. There are particular ways of doing things during math workshop. **Focus on math centers.** **Discuss using dominos.**	Transition to centers; engage in center work; practice working with a partner.	Center artifacts	Two games
13	How do we use math tools during math workshop?	There are certain routines that we practice during math workshop. There are particular ways of doing things during math workshop. **Focus on math workstations.** **Discuss math tools (counters, chips, rulers, etc.).**	Transition to centers; engage in center work; practice working with a partner.	Center artifacts	Two games

Figure 9.9 The First 20 Days of Guided Math *(continued)*

Day	Essential Questions	Big Ideas/Content	Skills	Assessments	Activities
14	What happens during the student work period during math workshop?	There are certain routines that we practice during math workshop. There are particular ways of doing things during math workshop. **Focus on guided math groups while other students work in centers.**	Follow schedule; practice working with a partner.	Center artifacts	Two games
15	What happens during the student work period during math workshop?	There are certain routines that we practice during math workshop. There are particular ways of doing things during math workshop. **Focus on guided math groups while other students work in centers.**	Follow schedule; practice working with a partner.	Center artifacts	Games/ Guided-math groups
Getting Started: Week 4					
Day	Essential Questions	Big Ideas/Content	Skills	Assessments	Activities
16	What happens during share time at the end of math workshop?	There are certain routines that we practice during math workshop. There are particular ways of doing things during math workshop. **Focus on share time.**	Sharing our work; reasoning out loud; modeling our thinking; listening to others	Teacher observation	Workshop schedule: Focus on class math journal; introduce Mathematician's Chair

Figure 9.9 The First 20 Days of Guided Math *(continued)*

			Teacher observation	Workshop schedule: Focus on class math journal; introduce Mathematician's Chair
17	What happens during Share Time at the end of Math Workshop?	There are certain routines that we practice during math workshop. There are particular ways of doing things during math workshop. **Focus on share time.**	Sharing our work; reasoning out loud; modeling our thinking; listening to others	
18	What are the routines, rules, and procedures during math workshop?	Spend these three days debriefing about how math workshop is going. Have the students draw pictures and write in their journals about math workshop. Talk about what is working well and what you need to change. This is the time to discuss and work out all the kinks. This is the blueprint for your yearlong journey. This period also gives you a few more days to spend on areas as you see fit. Every class is different. Consistency is the key!		
19	What are the routines, rules, and procedures during math workshop?			
20	What are the routines, rules, and procedures during math workshop?			

Summary

Math workshop is always a work in progress. It is a good idea to evaluate your workshop at the end of each unit of study so you can reflect on what went really well and what you will do differently next time. You can think about and reassess the mini-lessons (the books, poems, and songs); the various anchor charts and how effective they were; all of the math centers for that particular unit of study (were they engaging enough? were they rigorous enough? were they differentiated enough?); and the share sessions (did you really discuss all the math that you wanted your students to learn?). It is also a good idea to try and visit your colleagues' math workshops to see how they are going. How are they similar to or different from yours? Math workshop is a great adventure, full of new and wonderful surprises every day.

Reflection Questions to Ask Yourself After Each Week

1. What went really well?
2. What would you change?
3. What do the students still need to work on?
4. Are the anchor charts effective? How do you know?
5. How are your mini-lessons going? Are they engaging?
6. How smooth are the transitions throughout the workshop?
7. Are you really discussing the "Big Ideas" of the unit of study during the share?

Blackline Masters

Fact Sheets

Name: _____ Date: _____	Name: _____ Date: _____
Fact:	Fact:
Misconceptions/Errors:	Misconceptions/Errors:
Skills:	Skills:
Notes:	Notes:
Name: _____ Date: _____	Name: _____ Date: _____
Fact:	Fact:
Misconceptions/Errors:	Misconceptions/Errors:
Skills:	Skills:
Notes:	Notes:
Name: _____ Date: _____	Name: _____ Date: _____
Fact:	Fact:
Misconceptions/Errors:	Misconceptions/Errors:
Skills:	Skills:
Notes:	Notes:
Name: _____ Date: _____	Name: _____ Date: _____
Fact:	Fact:
Misconceptions/Errors:	Misconceptions/Errors:
Skills:	Skills:
Notes:	Notes:

Guided Math Lesson

Lesson Title: _____

Date: _____

Teaching Focus:
Math Vocabulary:
Activation/Previewing Activity:
Beginning of Lesson (Launch):
Middle of Lesson (Student Activity):
End of Lesson (Debrief):
Lesson:

Guided Math Plans

Group: _____   Dates: _____   Strategy Focus: _____

	Monday	Tuesday	Wednesday	Thursday	Friday
Introduction of Lesson					
Student Activity					
Debrief					
Next Steps					
Observation Notes					

Guided Math Record (A)

Dates:	Students:
Word Problem Type:	Teaching Points and Notes:

Dates:	Students:
Word Problem Type:	Teaching Points and Notes:

Dates:	Students:
Word Problem Type:	Teaching Points and Notes:

Dates:	Students:
Word Problem Type:	Teaching Points and Notes:

Dates:	Students:
Word Problem Type:	Teaching Points and Notes:

Dates:	Students:
Word Problem Type:	Teaching Points and Notes:

Guided Math Record (B)

Name:		

Goals:		Strength:

Date	Observation and Instruction	Next Steps to Meet Goal

Guided Math Sheet

Lesson Title: _____   Date: _____

Student	Observations

Record of Problem Solving

Student Name: _____

Problem Type	Observations

References

Calkins, L. (2001). *The art of teaching reading.* White Plains, NY: Longman.

Chapin, S. H., O'Connor, C., & Anderson, N. C. (2009). *Classroom discussions: Using math talk to help students learn, grades K–6* (2nd ed.). Math Solutions.

Collins, K. (2004). *Growing readers: Units of study in the primary classroom.* York, ME: Stenhouse.

Common Core State Standards for Mathematics. (2010). National Governors Association Center for Best Practices, Council of Chief State School Officers. Washington D.C. Retrieved from http://www.corestandards.org/assets/CCSSI_Math%20Standards.pdf.

De Corte, E., Verschaffel, L., & Op't Eynde, P. (2000). Self-regulation: A characteristic and a goal of mathematics learning. In M. Boekaerts, P. Pintrich, and M. Zeidner (Eds.), *Handbook of self-regulation* (pp. 687–747). San Diego: Academic Press.

Exemplars. (2012). Retrieved from www.exemplars.com.

Fountas, I. C., & Pinnell, G. S. (2001). *Guiding readers and writers: Grades 3–6.* Portsmouth, NH: Heinemann.

Gardner, H. (1983). *Frames of mind: The theory of multiple intelligences.* New York: Basic Books.

Harvey, S., & Goudvis, A. (2000). *Strategies that work: Teaching comprehension to enhance understanding.* York, ME: Stenhouse.

Katz, L. G., & Chard, S. C. (2000). *Engaging children's minds: The project approach* (2nd ed.). Stamford, CT: JAI Press. (ED456892).

Kohn, A. (1996). *Beyond discipline: From compliance to community.* Alexandria, VA: ASCD.

McIntosh, M. (2009). *Teachers—Formative assessment—Informal assessment of students' mathematical dispositions.* Retrieved from http://ezinearticles.com/?Teachers---Formative-Assessment---Informal-Assessment-of-Students-Mathematical-Dispositions&id=2177500.

Merz, A. (2009). Teaching for mathematical dispositions as well as for understanding: The difference between reacting to and advocating for dispositional learning. *Journal of Educational Thought, 43*(1), 65–78.

Mulgrave, C. (2011). Personal communication.

National Council of Teachers of Mathematics (NCTM). (1989). *Curriculum and evaluation standards for school mathematics.* Reston, VA: National Council of Teachers of Mathematics.

National Council of Teachers of Mathematics (NCTM). (2000). *Principles and standards for school mathematics.* Reston, VA: NCTM.

National Research Council. (2001). *Adding it up.* www.nap.edu/books/0309069955/html/.

Newton, R. (2010). Guided math presentations.

Opitz, M. (1998). *Flexible grouping in reading.* New York: Scholastic.

Perkins, D. (2003). *Making thinking visible.* Retrieved from http://pzweb.harvard.edu/vt/VisibleThinking_html_files/06_AdditionalResources/MakingThinkingVisible_DP.pdf.

Polya, G. (1957). *How to solve it* (2nd ed.). Princeton, NJ: Princeton University Press.

Resnick, L. B. (1999, June 16). Making America smarter. *Education Week Century Series. 18*(40), 38–40. Retrieved from: http://www.edweek.org/ew/vol-18/40resnick.h18.

Sibberson, F., & Szymsick, K. (2008). *Day-to-day assessment in the reading workshop.* New York: Scholastic.

Tomlinson, C. (1995). *How to differentiate instruction in the mixed ability classroom.* Alexandria, VA: ASCD.

Tomlinson, C. (2001). *How to differentiate instruction in mixed-ability classrooms* (2nd ed.). Alexandria, VA: ASCD.

Tomlinson, C. (2003). *Fulfilling the promise of the differentiated classroom: Strategies and tools for responsive teaching.* Alexandria, VA: ASCD.

Tomlinson, C., & Eidson C. (2003). *Differentiation in practice: A resource book for differentiating curriculum: Grades K–5.* Alexandria, VA: ASCD.

U.S. Department of Education. (2008). *Foundations for success: The final report of the National Advisory Panel.* Retrieved from http://www2.ed.gov/about/bdscomm/list/mathpanel/report/final-report.pdf.

Vygotsky, L. S. (1978). Mind in society: The development of higher psychological processes. *Interaction between learning and development* (pp. 79–91). Cambridge, MA: Harvard University Press.

Willis, Scott. (1993). "Teaching Young Children: Educators Seek 'Developmental Appropriateness.'" *Curriculum Update*, November, pp. 1–8.